The Blueprint:
Success is a State of Mind

By L. Fuchs

Dedication

This book is dedicated to my husband Victor Fuchs, who in his own way inspired and motivated me to stay on purpose and follow my dreams, and our children Lawrence and Elizabeth who are my pride and joy, and by far my greatest achievements, and to Prince Mikey the Monkey our non-human primate child and Louie, Angie and Annie our furry babies, who make my life complete.

Cover and Chapter Illustration Copyright © 2013 by Josh Porter
Cover Design by Rex Amarillo
Book Design, Layout and Production by Zeny St. George

Published by:
Lana Fuchs, LLC.
2330 Paseo Del Prado, Suite C101
Las Vegas, NV 89102
email@BuildABlueprint.com

ISBN 978-0-9891352-0-7

"I am always fascinated by the personal journey and lessons learned by a person. Your purpose for the book being to share those lessons in the hopes that the reader would in turn use them to inspire their own journey—Lana, on this you have delivered! I found myself taking copious notes, highlighting sentences, underlining, putting exclamation points in the margins, etc. The book has touched my life in a positive way in just the few short days I have had it and I have no doubt I will be reading it over and over again."

~**Jana Johnson**
Professor of Accounting, Finance, & Economics
University of Phoenix

"An easily understood written expose' of how quantum physics simply intersects with our physical reality. The author's love for the whole being and desire to generate a greater awareness of human maintenance is divinely accomplished with this book."

~ **Zannah Hackett, Ph.D.**
Founder
The Y.O.U. Institute

"[...] easy to read, follow and sharp [...] super controversial - but catches your attention for sure. It's my new bible!"

~**Larissa Goldberg**
Event Planner & Accreddited Bridal Consultant
Design by Larissa Events

"Many ancient scripts and notes can be calculated in between the lines of [Lana's] book. At times [Lana] address[es] some serious issues that will Bend hard-core religious zealots and Organized Church-folk. Stating that GOD is merely an acronym G.O.D - Great Omnipotent Designer will spin some heads - yet [Lana] actually treated that subject from [her] perspective so the majority of hard-core Jesus-Freaks or religious folks may have a few words to exchange. I believe the vision boards, positive affirmations are very tangible - but the true key: Conceive - Believe - Achieve is a tough pill for many to swallow and [Lana] discusses this notion very briefly - I hope the reader grasps the larger concept and its amazing, almost miraculous conquest. The book was a read smooth and rarely did I need my trusty dictionary."

~Dan McEllhattan III
Professor of Graphic Design
College of Southern Nevada

"The Blueprint is unique and special, and speaks about how to be successful and wealthy. A great book with suggestions that you can use immediately in your life. Lana Fuchs details everything with step-by-step instructions and life lessons on being successful. I would recommend this book to anyone and everyone."

~Sandra Johnson
Fare Media Agent
Metropolitan Transit Authority
Houston, TX

Acknowledgments

Once in a while this planet is blessed
When special souls come to be her guests
They all work tirelessly day and night
So that we could share with the world
The Blueprint of Light

These amazing people inspire me every day
In their own inconspicuously special way
They are my very own angels, teachers and guides
And are all beautiful spirits with brilliant minds

Master of the game, keeper of the scroll
I am here to help people rediscover their soul
But G.O.D knew that I couldn't do it alone
So it sent me my angels to help achieve my goal

I thank you all from the bottom of my heart
For having faith in The Blueprint
from the very start
Our journey together has only just begun
And I look forward to our future filled with
success,
wealth and lots of fun!

~Lana

Tracey Smith aka Tracey Baltimore, my business partner and soul sister. *Ryan Chapple*, my brother and friend and my son's Guardian Angel. *Dr. Zannah Hackett*, a brilliant and beautiful woman and my very own Fairy Godmother. *Josh Porter*, our resident genius and gifted artist whose opinion I respect immensely. *Rex Amarillo*, our very talented designer and graphic artist who oversees all design projects. *Zeny St. George*, our guru and all around brilliant mind who always achieves extraordinary results. *Tai Shane*, my makeup artist who always keeps me looking beautiful and entertained. *Herb Coleman, Vi'Ance Easter and Joseph "Joe" Alley*, our executive security who always keep us safe. *Freddy Ruano and Mara DeLeon*, my angels at home who always take care of my family and me. *Chloe St. George*, our youngest adviser and book expert.

I am grateful to each and every one of you for being in my life. Thank you for all your hard work, dedication, commitment and wisdom.

A special thank you to Renee Hertzler for sharing her life story, which inspired me to finish this book.

In special loving memory of Fanya Tulchinsky, my beautiful, kind and very wise grandmother, who has always been my biggest inspiration and number one fan! I miss her every day more than words can express.

The Blueprint:
Success is a State of Mind

By L. Fuchs

Foreword

The Blueprint: Success is a State of Mind

Success is a state of mind and knowledge is power...it all starts with The Blueprint. Many people ask me what makes me who I am and why I appear to be different. It's simple. I am who I am! I know myself and why I'm here and most importantly, I understand The Blueprint and the mechanics of the universe. There is an unseen world that few are aware of and this world has a natural order. This natural order is the working mechanism through which everything was created. Once you understand this mechanism, you can apply it in your own world to create a life of health, wealth, love, and perfect self-expression. This blueprint is a model and detailed plan of action that provides guidance to using the tools that you already have to get what you want. This is my secret power that works 100% of the time without fail, and I am about to share it with you.

I know Myself. Therefore, I know G.O.D. Thus I have power and I know how to use it! Do you know who you are? Are you ready to meet your true self and discover who you really are and what you can do?

Who are you?
Where did you come from?
Why are you here?

Why are some people fabulously wealthy while others are starving?
Why do some people have everything and some have absolutely nothing?
How do you achieve success in life?

If you're like most people, then you may have asked yourself these questions at least once or twice. If you haven't, well then perhaps you should. What if you were never told the truth about your origins and instead, have been manipulated and lied to? What if you were taught that you are powerless and you are not? What if you were programmed to believe that life is about hardship and struggle, when in fact it is your birthright to live a life of joy and abundance? What if only a few privileged and elite individuals had access to certain sacred knowledge that enabled them to amass great wealth and acquire unlimited power, at your expense? Could this be possible? You bet it is. Yes my friends, you have been deceived. If you choose freedom and truth, then this book is for you! If you want to continue living in darkness and suffer, then please do not read any further. If you want it all, then I invite you to open your minds and embark on this great adventure with me.

This book is a collection of lessons from my own personal journey of self-discovery and these are the principles I live by and use to design and create my life. Everything in this book is proven and verifiable and guaranteed to work 100% of the time without fail. It is also logical and to the point. The Blueprint is a universal technology that I used to put my marriage back together after a brutal, year-long separation from my husband along with a vicious legal battle. I used it to overcome disease and even to beat death. Seven years ago I was given a medical "diagnosis" and was told I had three weeks left to live. I told the doctor that I cannot and will not accept this ridiculous life sentence. I then told him to kiss my fabulous booty and proceeded to fix myself. Within a short period of time, I went to a different doctor for a "check-up" and of course, was told that I was in perfect health. It is also the same technology I used to create a life of abundance and prosperity, and continue to use every single day in every way.

When people see Lana Fuchs, they see the Lamborghini, the diamonds, the money, the glitz, and the glam, however life wasn't always that easy for me. As an immigrant child, I was an outcast, ignored, teased, and underestimated. I worked hard to get everything I have, so I make sure to live life to the fullest. I deny myself nothing! However, I've never forgotten my past, and when I found my power and my purpose, I knew that I would spend my life helping others find theirs. People say one person can't change the world. Well I say I can, one person at a time. I am living proof that anything is possible!

With this book, I give you infinite possibilities and I hope to inspire you to become enlightened and empowered so that you can create and live the life you want. I'm simply giving you The Blueprint and showing you how to use the tools you possess to create your own reality and express the fullest potential of human possibilities. Everything exists in the infinite field of probabilities, including the life you want. I'm not an expert or a guru. I am a student of life and I share with the world what I learn. I hope you're ready, because we are about to embark on an amazing journey of self-discovery.

"May the light restore your sight."

~Lana Fuchs

Please read this book in the order it was written because each chapter builds and creates various layers producing a multidimensional blueprint. Every time you read this book, you will discover something new.

party for any loss, damage, or disruption caused by errors or omissions, whether such errors or omissions result from negligence, accident, or any other cause.

This book is not intended as a substitute for the medical advice of physicians. The reader should regularly consult a physician in matters relating to his/her health and particularly with respect to any symptoms that may require diagnosis or medical attention.

Contents

The Story of Creation

And so the story begins
of how this planet came to be
The story of creation,
of them, of you, and me...

At one boundless cosmic point,
before there was a time
When there was only space,
so vast and so sublime
The spirit and the source of all,
the omnipotent and divine
In all his splendor and magnificence,
the Mighty Mastermind

So overflowing was he
with beauty, love, and light
That he experienced a feeling
of pure rapture and sheer delight
Thus born was the desire to share
this love with a being of like mind
And so a thought was formed
to create another of his kind

Now the Great Creator, so blissful and inspired
In his grand design, a partner he desired
Illuminated with his resplendent light
and bursting from within
He would not contain himself, eager to begin

From his divine excitement, a tiny spark flew down

And thus was born the Consciousness of Love,
wearing his radiant crown
With his beloved partner, the Great Creator spoke,
"Tell me Love," he said, "Who first shall we evoke?"

Love replied, "My dear Divine Creator,
what do you foresee
Will be created from the union
between you and me?"
To this the Great Creator,
replied with joy and glee,
"But don't you see my Love,
they'll be like you and me!"

"They'll be exquisite, radiant and divine;
we'll call them humankind.
I'll give them wisdom, courage, strength,
and each a brilliant mind!
They shall also have free will,
and the genius to create
Each one will be the Master
of his and her own fate."

"I want them to be happy, so in my image,
I shall make them god-like
And you my Love, will gift them with your beauty
and your charm; no two will be alike.
I'll also give them passion,
and you will give them grace
And when they feel and express their love,
it shall show on each face.

Each of our beloved offspring
shall possess a special light
And when they are in harmony,
we'll see them shine so bright."
Love listened to her revered Creator and
asked him once again,
"Yes, but in return for all these gifts,
what will you expect of them?"

The Great Creator pondered,
and then began to speak,
He said, "It's just their love I want,
that's all I'll ever seek."
Love then understood the Great Creator's needs
And began growing for him,
her special loving seeds

She contemplated the great task
that lay ahead of them,
"Well then," she said,
"we'll need guides and teachers
if they create mayhem."
So the Great Creator imaged for his kin
Magnificent celestial spirits,
and called them Seraphim.

He said, "Very well my Love,
I've done as you have asked."
And in the Angels' dazzling light,
his Lady Love was basked.
The ever-loving mother said,
"My sweet, just one more thing,"
I want our sons and daughters to live in a place

fit for a queen and king."
The Great Creator studied,
the cosmos far and wide
He even asked the Seraphim and
Lady Love to help him to decide
What place would be deemed worthy
for his cherished descendants to reside.

A location has been chosen,
not too far away from home
Where their divine children will be sent
to experience and roam
To learn and feel, and then return
where they'll be happy, safe, and warm
So that they can rest and study,
and obtain a brand new form

These two majestic beings then merged
and became as one
Surrounded by the singing angels,
that's how life had begun.
When our divine ascendants united to procreate
The euphoria they experienced
was designed for us to duplicate
So that our beautiful planet
we may continue to populate.

From that moment forward
all those who merge in love
Experience the same pleasure
as our ancestors from above.
So this is how it came to be
that humankind was born

And I was presented with my first birthday gift,
a majestic unicorn

I rode him bareback with my hair flying
in the gentle breeze
While my mate was chasing me
with agility and ease
How happy we were then, how blissful and carefree
Running, playing, and frolicking; just him and me.
Those of you who read this might ask,
"What about the tree?"

The tree is a mere symbol of foolishness and greed
That still destroys our planet and our entire breed
Even now the Great Creator,
along with Mother Love
Are watching us and crying, silently above.

But just like any parents, they want the best for us,
And hope and wish that we would learn,
and in them we trust.

The Blueprint

Chapter 1
G.O.D - Great Omnipotent Designer
DNA of Success

The Blueprint

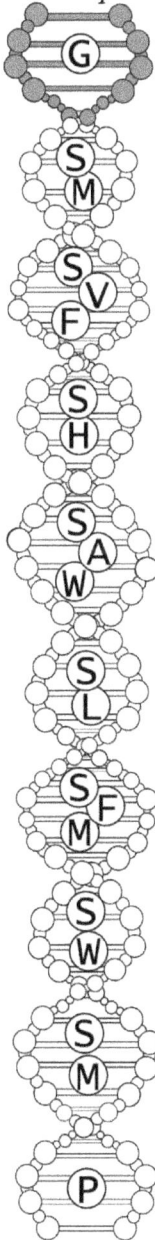

The Blueprint

There is an unseen world that few are aware of and this world has a Blueprint of a natural order and a working mechanism through which it was created. This ancient and elegant design is responsible for all of creation. Once you understand this mechanism, you can use it to create your world in much the same way. This mechanism is complex in its simplicity. People tend to complicate things and then take great pride and pleasure in being able to explain and break it down to others. In reality, it is not only simple; it's already a part of your DNA. This is nothing more than a reminder of what you already know on a cellular level. Let's go back in time to the beginning and the source from where everything originates, including you and me. Creation is the game we play. Replication is the name of this game.

The Origins of Everything

In the beginning before creation, before the Bible, before television, before everything, there was the cosmos, which was pure consciousness. This consciousness, consisting of male and female energy was self-aware, but it did not have form or pattern. The energy of the consciousness was made up of layers within layers of waveforms and cosmic

8

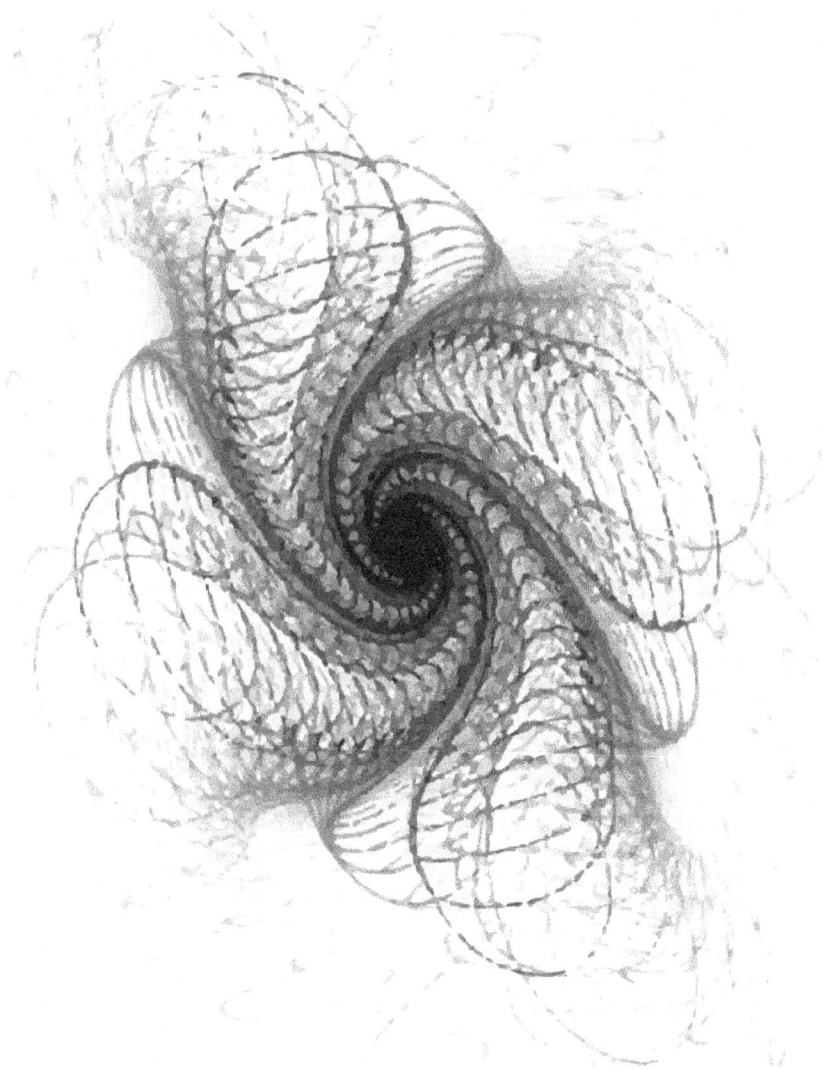

G.O.D (Great Omnipotent Designer) is consciousness of pure potential, consisting of waveforms within waveforms, and cosmic foam. These waveforms are probabilities of everything that may or may not ever happen.

foam, which are probabilities of everything that may or may not ever happen. It was pure potential. This is what many people think of as God, Goddess, Infinite Intelligence, Source, Tao, and many others. I prefer to think of it as Great Omnipotent Designer or G.O.D.

At some point, the cosmos or G.O.D had a thought which had unlimited potential and possibilities. This thought was living energy, and it burst out into countless directions and infinite dimensions. In an instant, our entire universe was imagined, from the tiniest bacteria to human beings, and everything in between. In order to maintain the perfect balance and harmony of the cosmos, thought sealed itself off by focusing inward. This created a donut shaped bubble, which became our world. At this point, G.O.D consciousness surrounded and covered our universe like a protective blanket, forming a border between our world and infinity. Now there is a perfect playground for physical life to evolve.

G.O.D's thought was the cause, and our universe is the effect. G.O.D created our universe by its thought and then focused on certain waveforms and turned them into particles or matter. G.O.D's attention held and continues to hold the particles together to sustain its creation. Everything around us is energy and is constantly vibrating, so the matter, which makes up our universe only looks solid, but in reality it's not. The other waveforms of probability that G.O.D did not focus on and since they weren't getting any attention, simply collapsed. The collapsed

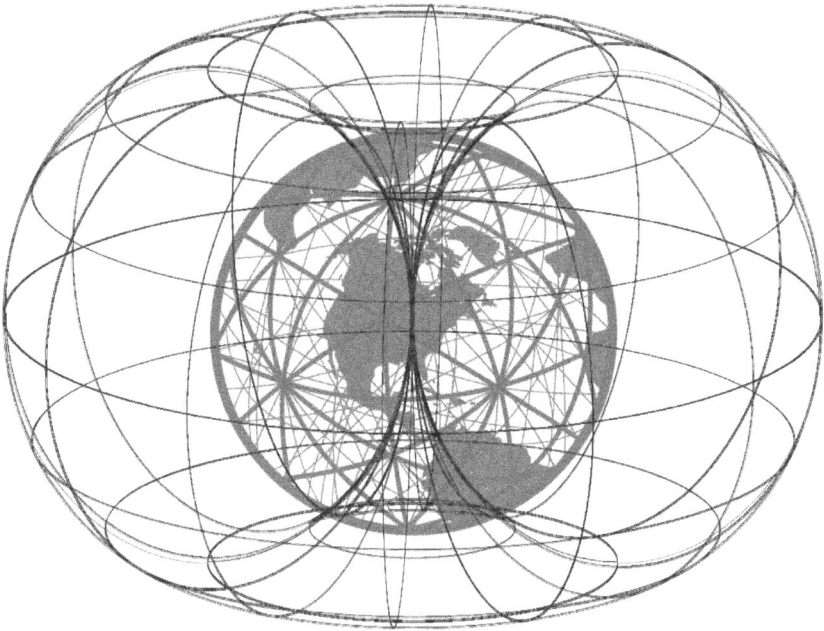

G.O.D's thought and attention is the cause of our donut shaped universe, which is the effect.

waveforms didn't disappear. In fact nothing ever disappears. Everything always exists as a probability. This is really important to know, because we create our own reality in exactly the same way. Whatever we think about, focus on, and pay attention to is what happens in our physical world. Our emotions and willpower fuel our thoughts and propel them into existence.

Let's look at this again because this is the mechanism for the creation of anything and everything. G.O.D's thought and perception determined which waveforms would turn into particles and form something, and which would not. G.O.D's attention held and continues to hold its thought in place. We are the result and creation of G.O.D's thought. However if G.O.D decided to no longer pay attention to our universe, it would soon fall apart and cease to exist. Understanding this process is vital to creating our own reality. Whatever we think about and focus on takes shape and happens. What we pay attention to continues to exist simply because we're paying attention to it. What we don't focus on or pay attention to loses its energy and ceases to exist in the physical world. Our imagination and our thoughts create our emotions, fuel our creations, and our willpower propels them into existence. Our attention keeps our creations in place.

When G.O.D had this thought, it imagined and envisioned every detail and organizational mechanism needed to shape and sustain our world. For physical life to evolve, we needed space, time, energy, and mass. To sustain our universe, we needed the four fundamental forces: gravity, electromagnetism, and strong and weak nuclear force. Thus we have potential for physical life and limitless evolution.

Let There Be Self Expression

So now we have a playground, and we're ready for children, animals, plants, and all kinds of life. When G.O.D, which is like Mother-Father consciousness, focused its attention on certain waveforms, it turned them into mass, and this is what scientists might refer to as the Big Bang. I think of it as a cosmic orgasm. It sounds more exciting to me than the big bang. We can compare it to our own orgasm. When we climax, we have that delicious, pulsating feeling of a big bang, which expands and contracts, and energy explodes from within us, along with certain bodily fluids. We basically mimic the cosmic orgasm. In fact, most of life on this planet is designed to emulate the cosmic orgasm. Hence we have reproduction. It is a brilliant mechanism, because without the orgasm I don't know that we would ever reproduce.

During the cosmic orgasm, just like our bodies, the interior of our universe expanded, and echoes or fragments of G.O.D consciousness attached themselves to the particles streaming out of the cosmic orgasm. Now we have countless, individualized viewpoints and life in various physical forms. Thus G.O.D has an infinite amount of physical bodies to live and learn in, and experience through. As time passed, creation became more complex as particles connected with one another based on the organizational mechanism created by G.O.D and set into motion by its child, our universe. What is really amazing is that all these particles come equipped with their own fragment of G.O.D consciousness and their own intelligence. These particles are the building blocks of our universe.

Each G.O.D particle is equally important with its own purpose, and knows what role it needs to play as a part of our universe. At each level of creation and evolution, G.O.D particles become more sophisticated in their ability to make choices and manage their existence. The more complex an organism becomes, the less of them exist in creation. Through evolution, the presence of human beings was a reality. Along the line of the same principles, the more complex a human being is, the less of them exist.

We humans are an interesting species. Each human being is quite complex, with a governing Oversoul G.O.D particle (oG.O.D), which is pure intelligence and is aware of cosmic unity. Then below there is the Ego G.O.D particle (eG.O.D), which typically lives in a world of illusion and believes that it is separated from everyone and everything else. It's the selfish part of each one of us that is annoying and sometimes difficult to handle. Oftentimes there is a conflict between the oG.O.D and the eG.O.D in the decision making process. The oG.O.D will make decisions based on the greatest good for the greatest number, while the eG.O.D will only care about itself, without any regard to how the consequences of its actions will affect everyone and everything else. It's kind of like having an angel on one shoulder and a demon on the other. I'm sure we've all seen cute pictures depicting this scenario.

Fortunately, our universe is sealed off from G.O.D, and what happens in our universe is theoretically contained here. We can look at it like this. G.O.D is the Mother-Father in their home and our universe is the child in his own room, and what the child does in his room, doesn't really affect the environment in the parents' house. So if the child makes a mess in his room, leaves his toys everywhere, and doesn't make the bed, the parents' house, for the most part is still nice and intact. The child has his or her own space and it's up to the child to demonstrate that he or she appreciates and respects their space and takes care of it.

However if the child starts a fire in their room, there is a good chance that the whole house may burn down, and possibly even the neighbors' houses. If that occurs, the parents can send in older, responsible siblings or a nanny-babysitter to ensure the safety of the child, and everyone living in the house, as well as the next-door neighbors. This is pretty much the scenario with our universe. As long as we don't do anything to destroy our planet and our galaxy, and adversely affect all of creation, we can play in our own room or universe. Unfortunately the human race has gotten to such a high level of toxicity that it requires assistance. Human beings are acting like irresponsible children, making a serious mess on this planet and subjecting all of creation to potential harm. If these were my children, there would be serious consequences for them.

Are We Alone?

Since replication is the name of the game, G.O.D must have had more than one thought, so presumably there are other universes with other life forms and beings, which are also experiencing life within their levels of evolution. There are hierarchies on all levels of creation, and I believe that the human race is not at the top of that hierarchy. In fact, I believe humanity is very young and still has much to learn. Since all of creation is endowed with the imagination and the power to create, it is also possible that the human race was created by other intelligent life form. Regardless, we are all comprised of the exact same building blocks, G.O.D particles - Light.

What is Karma?

We all use the word karma and we all know that it basically means what you reap is what you sow. However, I think it's important for us to really understand where it comes from and how it works. It's quite simple actually. In the design of our universe, time flows downward through the middle of our world, which is our present time, and flows into our past as history. Karma is the consequence of the choices made in the present by every single G.O.D particle, and is the mechanism through which the consequences of choices and behavior determine the probabilities of our future.

Each G.O.D particle generates its own karma based on the choices it makes. Since it takes trillions of G.O.D particles to hold together every one of us that means all our G.O.D particles are responsible for creating our karma. We are all affected by one another's karma. The more a G.O.D particle has in common with another G.O.D particle, the more it is affected by the other's karma. Therefore, couples generate not only their individual karma, but also karma as a couple; as

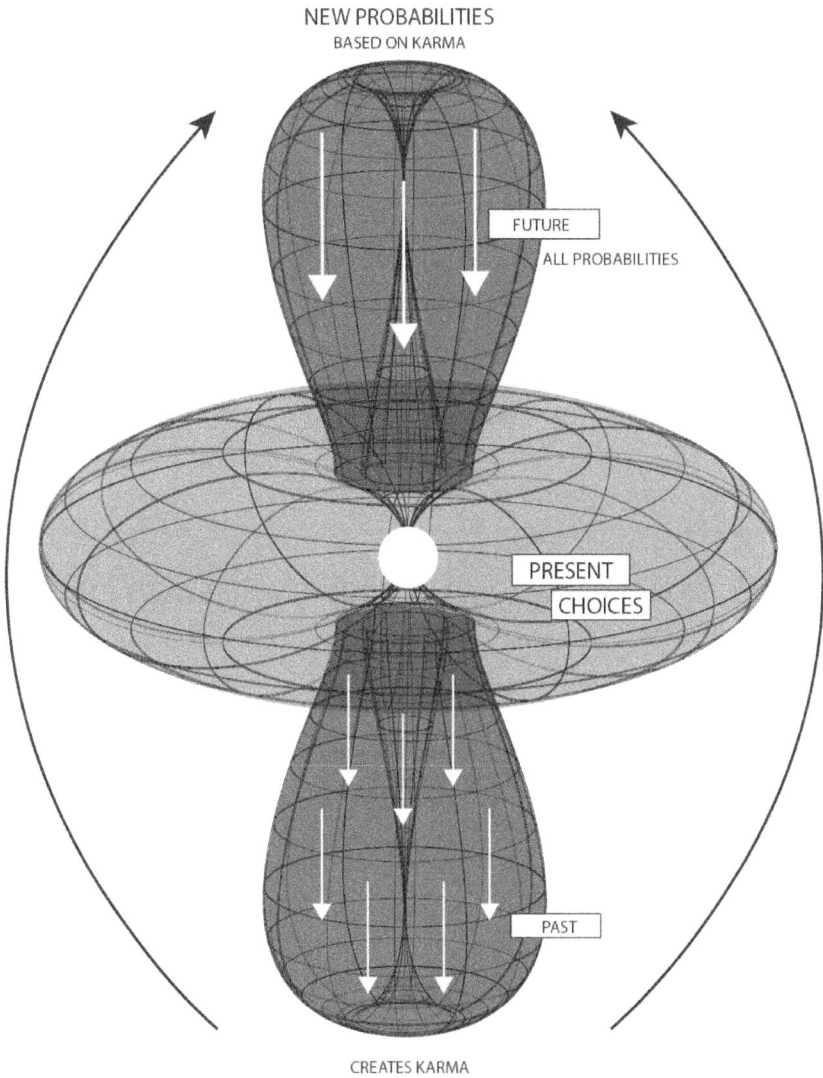

NEW PROBABILITIES
BASED ON KARMA

FUTURE
ALL PROBABILITIES

PRESENT
CHOICES

PAST

CREATES KARMA

In our universe time flows downward. Karma is the consequence of the choices made in the present, by every G.O.D particle and determines the probabilities of our future.

one unit. The same goes for families, companies, countries, societies, etc. Like a ripple effect, our collective karma affects all of creation.

What we perceive, we receive. We all consciously or unconsciously create our lives based on our thoughts, feelings, emotions, and perceptions. Some people do so consciously and intentionally, but the vast majority, create their lives unconsciously. Although we human beings prefer to blame someone or something outside of ourselves for what happens to us, it is all our own doing. Our lives are the sum total of the choices we make. So stop thinking of yourself as a victim and start looking at yourself as the ruler of your own galaxy and the master of your own fate. You can consciously and intentionally create and re-create every part of your life as often as you'd like.

What Is Reality?

Reality is such an interesting concept. What is reality? Have you ever thought about what that means? Well, what is real to me is not necessarily real to you and vice versa. While we all have the power to create our own individual realities, we all live within a single universal reality that we know of as our world. Let's explore our reality, or actually the virtual reality we live in.

Regardless of the size, complexity, or level of sophistication of the physical matter to which the G.O.D particles are attached, they don't have a size and they don't occupy a particular location.

Technically, we all live within a hyper-dimensional, electromagnetic, holographic universe that responds to our dominant thoughts and emotions, and plays back to us that which we are.

Think of it like playing a virtual reality game, in which we can articulate and express our creative energy utilizing our free will and unique individual perspective. When you're playing video games, you can be sitting on your couch at home and using the control panel to play the game and control your avatar, but your avatar is somewhere in the middle of a different country or perhaps in a different galaxy doing whatever you're making them do based on the rules and objectives of the game you're playing.

The electromagnetic universe we live in is completely interconnected to all life, like a cosmic internet grid, and every component is connected to each other and to everything else. Earth, our playground in this virtual reality game, like everything in creation is alive and vibrates on a certain frequency. We human beings are like vibrational transmitters, who constantly receive and transmit energy. Together, we tune Earth to our collective vibration.

There are two basic vibrations. They are fear and love. Currently, humanity lives in the low frequency of fear, and as a result we are unable to have clear connection to the grid and for the most part cannot communicate, travel, see, and interact with intelligent life from higher frequencies. The time has come for us to learn to manage our own energies and to raise our collective vibrational frequency. Stop giving away your power to anyone and everyone out there. Reclaim it for yourself. It's your birthright.

Overview

Are you beginning to put together the pieces of this puzzle? If so, you're beginning to re-member and reassemble yourself. Everything and everyone in our universe, reduced down to the most basic form, consists of the exact same single pure energy, which is light, vibrating on different frequencies...G.O.D particles, which connect with other G.O.D particles of the same harmonious frequency to form what we perceive as reality and shapes our physical world. Allow me to introduce you to yourself. If you want to meet G.O.D, look in the mirror. You hold The Blueprint of creation and cosmic power within yourself. Now it is time to learn how to use it to consciously and intentionally create your life.

Chapter 2
Success Creation Mechanism
The Blueprint

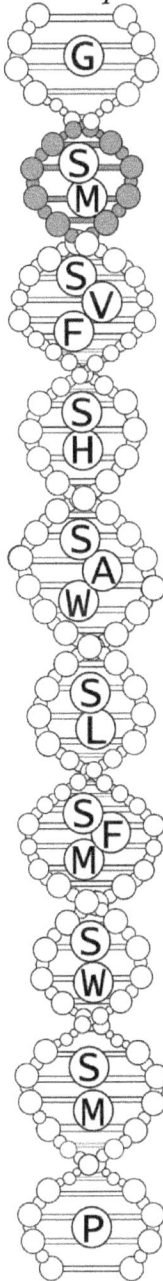

The Blueprint

Just as the ancients and masters have been saying for thousands of years, you are responsible for everything that happens in your life. You created it all whether you know it or not. Look closely at everything in your universe and realize that you are the designer and creator of your life. Your thoughts, feelings, emotions and perceptions created it all and the attention you keep placing on all the things in your life keeps it in place. I hope you like what you see. If you see a pattern of attraction to similar kinds of people or scenarios, you may want to look at that. In order to change your life, you must change your thoughts and perceptions. Everything begins in the mind.

That is how our world was designed to operate. Regardless of what you may currently believe to be true, you are not the victim of some external circumstances or events. You are the creator of your reality. You are the producer, director, and star of your own movie. If you want to change a scene in the movie or a character, or the entire movie for that matter, all you have to do is change the script. You are the writer of that script.

Your Reality

All of creation is comprised of waveforms that we transmute to particles simply by placing attention on them. Absolutely everything that may or may not happen exists as a probability, waiting for you to bring it to physical life. All you have to do is choose what you want and attract it to yourself by aligning your vibrational frequency with the frequency of what you want.

Energy or G.O.D particles share information with all other energy instantly, regardless of geographic or cosmic location. Everything is wired together on the cosmic grid so energy doesn't travel because it doesn't need to. All energy is already interconnected with all other energy. We are all ONE! Time and space are completely irrelevant. A projection of energy in Russia can and does affect energy in the U.S. and around the world instantaneously. Everything in the entire cosmos is nothing but a huge vibrating ball of interconnected infinite energy, which has the ability to communicate into infinity with no regard to space and time. What this energy joins together to form is based only on individual thought. So if the object of your desire is in a different city, state, or country, it doesn't matter. The only limits you have are those which are self imposed. You possess unlimited power, and when you consciously create your reality, the might of the universe is behind you.

Everything in creation is comprised of waveforms that we transmute into particles simply by placing our attention on them.

However, with great power comes great responsibility. If you can conceive and believe that your biggest goals, dreams, and desires can come true, they will. In fact, they can happen instantly. While this is an intoxicating thought, I must warn you that this power works both ways. If you believe on any level, whether consciously or subconsciously, that you will get a disease, perhaps because it is hereditary in your family, sooner or later, you will get this disease.

The Mechanism

Now that you are aware of your tremendous power, I bet you are ready to start using it. This is The Blueprint and mechanism behind this power. Your dominant thoughts and feelings are energy. You naturally project and broadcast this energy out into the universe constantly. It harmonizes with energy of the same frequency in waveforms and transmutes these waveforms into particles. These particles will attract additional particles that harmonize with it and create matter. This is how your thoughts and feelings become your physical reality. Whatever you think will happen and feel strongly about, will happen. You will be right 100% of the time.

Be aware, what you fear or resist the most, will happen because that's what you focus your attention on. Remember, what you resist persists. If you continue to resist it, you become it, marry it, or have it as a child. Fear is a very low vibration that makes people weak and subservient. Human beings generally tend to fear the unknown, and then once it becomes known, it is no longer a fear. If you understand that you possess unlimited power and create your own reality, fear becomes obsolete.

What you believe and feel to be true, regardless if those beliefs or feelings are based on real truth or perceived truth, is what will create your reality and will determine how your life unfolds. There is no such thing as an untruth, only your individual perception of truth. It is actually the act of observing an object, including events, conditions, and circumstances that cause it to be there. The outcome is based only on your choice and how you see it. An object cannot and does not exist independently of its observer. There is no objective reality.

You may think that there are various forms of energy, such as energy that powers your home, energy that powers your car, and energy that powers your body. It is in fact the same energy that powers absolutely everything and everyone, everywhere. The only difference is the vibrational frequencies that form the various constructs and structures. Everything that exists whether it is oxygen, stars, your five senses, electricity, money, sound, rain, your thoughts and emotions, your car, your physical body, your dog and your monkey, is comprised of this very same energy.

Are you ready to change your life now? Here is your very own magic wand and your every wish is its command. If at first, this appears to be a bit difficult, don't worry. It's not, and just like everything else, the more you use it the better you get at it. Practice makes permanent. Eventually you'll do it in a matter of minutes or seconds. Have faith in yourself. After all, you are G.O.D!

The Creation Blueprint

- Your dominant thoughts and feelings are energy.

- You naturally project and broadcast this energy out into the universe constantly.

- It then harmonizes with energy of a harmonious frequency in waveforms and transmutes these waveforms into particles.

- These particles will then attract additional particles that harmonize with it and create matter.

- This is how your thoughts and feelings become your physical reality. Whatever you think and feel strongly about, will happen.

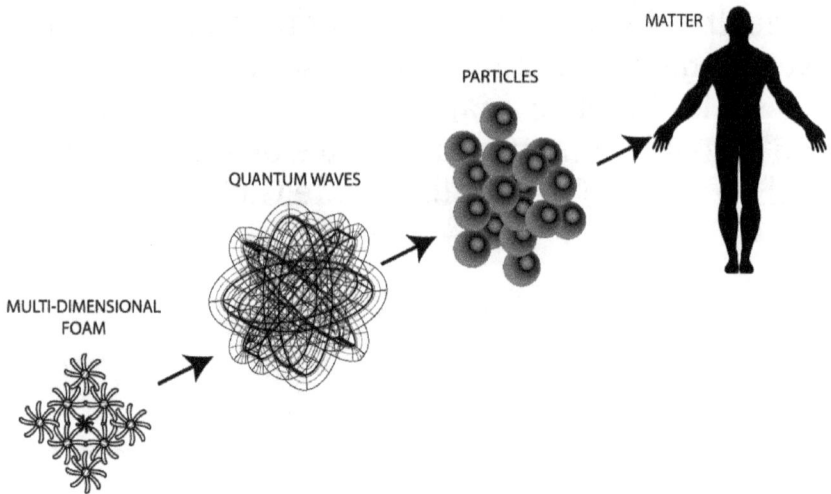

MATTER

PARTICLES

QUANTUM WAVES

MULTI-DIMENSIONAL
FOAM

When you think about what you choose to have in your universe, your thoughts are broadcast out into the cosmos, and with your emotions transform waves and foam into particles. They then attract other particles on a harmonious frequency and form physical matter. So, if you want to create the perfect man, or the perfect new you, or your perfect new house, this is the mechanism for creation. Everything in creation is made up of the exact same energy or G.O.D particles.

Overview

Everything that happens in your life is a result of how you think and what you believe, whether it's conscious or subconscious. Your perceptions are always the cause and your life is the effect. You can choose to remain as the mass majority

does, fully believing you are a victim of circumstance, or consciously align and harmonize your actions, thoughts, and beliefs with the greatest creative power in the universe and become a conscious creator of your life. It's your choice. Our universe is an electromagnetic, hyper-dimensional, virtual reality construct that responds to our thoughts, feelings, and emotions. This technology has been taught in certain spiritual circles and the most powerful secret societies since the beginning of time. This is sacred knowledge. You can use this knowledge to bring you almost everything you desire. To live life in harmony with yourself and your surroundings is the greatest experience in the cosmos. The soul indicates its desire, the mind chooses from its options, and the body acts out that choice. When all the G.O.D particles of the mind, body, and soul create together and are in harmony, G.O.D is made flesh. G.O.D wants to experience everything, so that it can be everything. We are constantly experiencing, evolving, and becoming. This is our purpose.

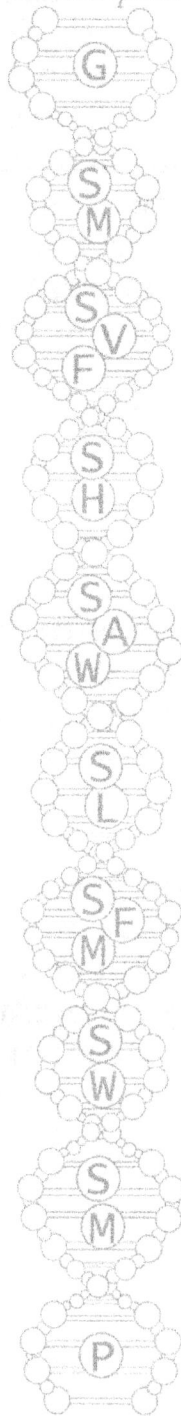

The Blueprint

Chapter 3
The Frequency of Success

The Blueprint

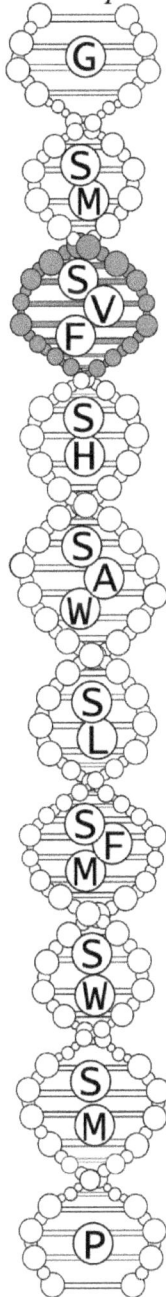

The Blueprint

Every human being is an electromagnetic vibrational transmitter and we live within an electromagnetic vibrational universe. Like a magnet, you naturally attract to yourself whatever and whoever is in harmony with who you are, and repel whatever or whoever is out of sync with you. If you energetically radiate health, you will get more health. If you radiate or project feeling old, you will attract more reasons to age. If you broadcast an abundance of wealth you will receive more wealth. If you broadcast the feeling of success, you will get more successes in your life. Are you getting the picture? Your physical reality reflects who you are. The universe does not pick and choose what to send you. Your vibration attracts compatible patterns. What you send out into the universe is what you get back from the universe. There is a boomerang effect. In order to change your life you must change the energetic patterns you're putting out.

Intended Purpose of Your Power

You have access to unlimited power. You've always had it, however up until now; many of you were not taught how to use it. The information is in your cellular memory and a part of your DNA and this is just a refresher course. It's not any different than driving a car. Imagine if someone gave you a brand new car, but did not tell you what it was or what it could do. You might look at this car and decide that it was beautiful, but if you did not know that it could actually move, it might end up as a cool piece of furniture.

Then, someone comes to visit and asks why you're using this car as furniture instead of driving it. You might look at this person like they are crazy because you didn't even know that this thing had an engine. Now imagine that you're getting into the driver's side and your guest gets into the passenger side and the fun begins! He shows you how to use your car key to turn on the engine. You can feel the power. Then, he takes you out on the open road and shows you how to drive it and what this car can really do. You're amazed! You've had this incredible power all this time but you were not utilizing it the way it was intended by the original builder and creator of the car. You're experiencing for the first time what I can only describe as a vehicular orgasm. You're getting this, right?

Well, now you drive this car all the time, everywhere and you've become somewhat of a driving expert. Some time later, you go visit another friend and in her house, you see a car, which also serves as a piece of furniture. You proceed, with great pride and joy, and perhaps a little bit of a superior attitude, to tell her that this is not furniture. This thing has power and it can transport you from one place to another. You then take your friend and her car out on the road, and do the same things your other friend did with you. Before you know it, all your friends and neighbors are driving their cars instead of using them as furniture and wasting all this power.

Start your engines! You are about to find out what you and your body can really do! You are the creator of your own universe. Through the study of science and spirituality, we can understand in great detail the mechanics of conscious intentional and unconscious unintentional creation of our own lives. Regardless of your religious preference, scientific knowledge, or level of education, you can use this information to design and construct your life. This book is The Blueprint and you already have within you all the tools you need.

Unlimited Power

Each and every person is endowed with the power of creation and we all create, whether we know it or not. There is, however, a difference in what we can create. Some people may need to do a little inner clean up or energy shifting prior to conscious creation. Your vibrational frequency is the determining factor in the amount of power you have. If an individual is vibrating on a lower frequency and is living in a general state of depression, anger, and fear, then such a person can only create his reality unconsciously. He can only by default attract to himself more of the same. If you are that person, don't worry. It is easily corrected by raising your frequency. Then you'll be able to consciously manifest positive things.

Do you know anyone who seems to live a magical and charmed life? Someone who lives in the lap of luxury and is always happy and healthy? This person seems to have it all. For example: health, wealth, good looks, and a glamorous life. Why do all these amazing things keep happening to this person? The answer is simple. It's because this person vibrates on a high frequency of health and wealth and is therefore attracting more of the same into their universe.

I'm sure there are also quite a few people you know who seem to go from one crisis to another. They are miserable, depressed, angry, and always worry about a lack of money. It seems like terrible things happen to them all the time. This is a constant way of life for them because they vibrate on a low frequency of fear, anxiety, and misery. Since like attracts like, they constantly attract more negative things to be upset about. These patterns will continue unless and until their frequency is changed.

I can compare this scenario to music. If you keep tuning into a radio station that predominantly plays hip-hop, but you are waiting and hoping that they will play classical music, then you're in for quite a disappointment. It's not going to happen. You are a vibrational transmitter, and like a magnet, you naturally attract whatever and whoever is in harmony with who you are, and repel whatever or whoever is out of sync with you.

The rich get richer and the poor get poorer; misery loves company, and the people you hang out with rub off on you. By the same token, those people who are used to living in mediocrity also attract more mediocrity. You attract to you what you feel and what you focus on with great emotion. People need to learn how to live as vibrational beings in a vibrational universe. Everything has a frequency and everyone has their own unique signature frequency. We are both transmitters and receivers of energy.

Your Frequency

Quiet your mind, tune in to yourself, and listen to your inner vibrational transmitter. What are you broadcasting? When I tune into myself, I sense that I am broadcasting positive energy and signals to attract perfect health, wealth and happiness into my life. I'm radiating happiness, fulfillment, and an abundance of wealth. I know that my energy is intellectual at the moment because I'm writing this book. I would describe this frequency as flowing, warm, sweet, smiling, happy, peaceful, soaring, green, soft, energized and powerful with a sexy sweet aroma.

I can also tune into the vibrations from my environment. I can sense that my body is broadcasting youth, health, and power. I feel that it's cool and crisp outside. I hear my daughter as she is doing her homework next to me. I see Mikey the Monkey curiously examining his remote control toy. Overall, I can feel that my vibration is in sync and in perfect harmony with my environment. This is a pretty constant and stable frequency for me. It's important to understand that your frequency affects your thoughts and emotions. If you change the energy you are broadcasting, your thoughts and feelings will change too. That in turn will change your perception of life and what you perceive, you receive.

Raising Your Vibrational Frequency

There are different ways to raise your frequency. These are some of my favorites.

1. **A Quick Pick-Me-Up:** This is a great one for a quick fix. It works in just a few seconds. Get up, move around, jump up and down, take a brisk walk, or better yet take your pet for a walk (if you have one), go for a swim, twirl, dance, or listen to your favorite happy song. This will revive and raise your frequency for a short time. It's also very useful if you're around someone who is vibrating on a very low frequency and you feel like the energy has been sucked out of you. I think we all know a few people like that. They're just energetically heavy and bring you down.

2. **Permanent But Gradual:** If you're interested in permanently raising your frequency and

changing your life, but doing it gradually, this one's for you. Here is how this works. It's basically daydreaming. Vividly imagine and visualize what you want for 15 to 30 minutes at least once every day. Visualize in such a way that you can feel strong emotions. An emotional change indicates that you're broadcasting a new frequency. The longer you can hold this new vibration, the faster your physical reality will change. Once you start transmitting a new frequency, you will repel whatever and whoever in your life is incompatible with your new vibration, and soon, you will begin attracting those people and experiences that are compatible with your new vibration. If you maintain the new vibration long enough, you'll see your whole physical reality change all around you.

3. **I Want It All and I Want It Now!** For the fastest and most effective way to raise your vibrational frequency and improve your life, you must intentionally disconnect from the energetic patterns you're compatible with by changing the dominant frequency you're broadcasting. This means you must change completely as much in your life as possible. Remember, you are both a transmitter and receiver of energy. Since you're constantly receiving energy from your environment, you have to change it.

It's not as difficult as you think although it does require courage and willpower. You have to want it! If you have friends who are lazy, miserable and have a false sense of entitlement, banish them. This also applies to people you are dating. Instead find people who are happy with their lives and are productive. Don't watch or feed into the latest "financial meltdown" in the news, and do not watch horror movies or engage in any low vibrational frequency activities. Instead, read inspirational and uplifting books about successful, self-made people. Music affects your frequency in a major way, so I suggest listening to high vibrating, uplifting music, such as Chopin. Spend more time outdoors in nature, because it is the fastest and easiest way to cleanse your energy and raise your frequency.

It may feel strange and uncomfortable at first because you are not yet compatible with this new frequency, but eventually you'll start to integrate this new energy, and your own vibrational pattern will soon adjust and harmonize with the new frequency in your life. Have fun with this technology. The only limits are self-imposed. Be brave and daring. Go for your dreams!

Vibrational Stability

Your vibrational being and your environment will tend to stabilize over time. If your current life situation appears fairly stable, it's safe to say that you're maintaining stability. For example, if you're

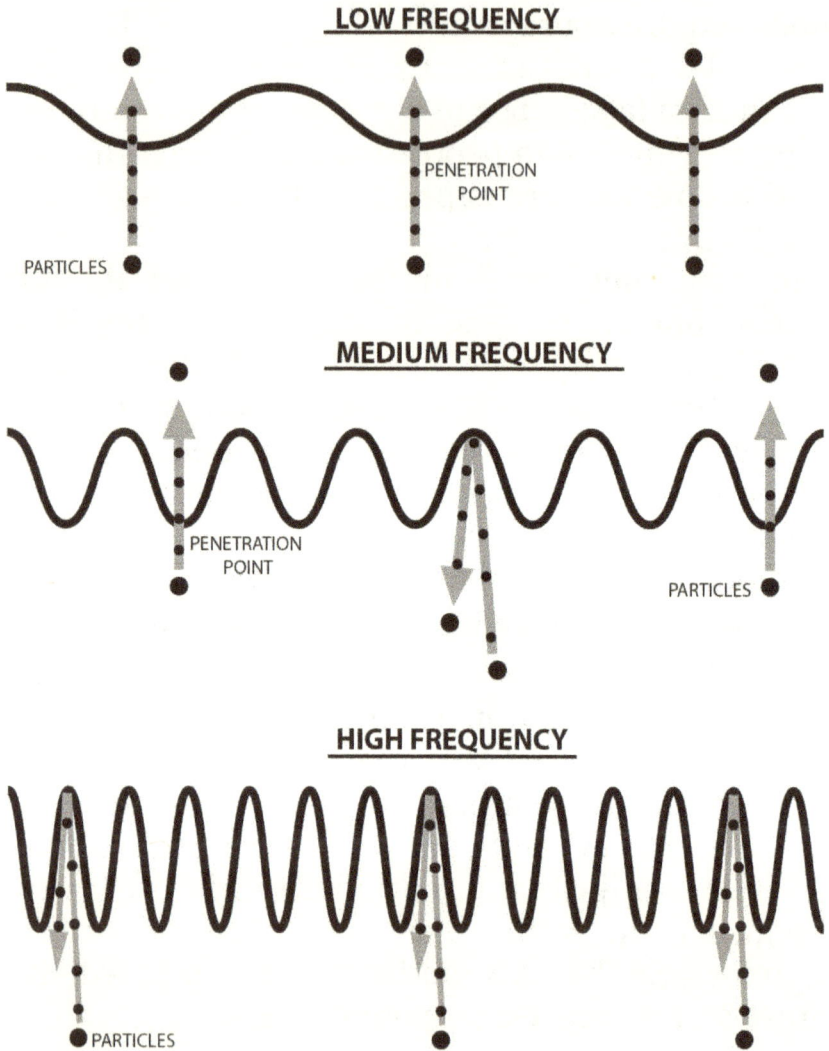

LOW FREQUENCY

PENETRATION POINT

PARTICLES

MEDIUM FREQUENCY

PENETRATION POINT

PARTICLES

HIGH FREQUENCY

PARTICLES

The low frequency is vey weak and vulnerable and is open to any comparable low vibrating energies such as illness, poverty, fear and anger. The medium frequency is stronger and healthier and will leave you less vulnerable but still in a position of weakness. The high vibrating energy will keep you protected from the unwanted energies and will keep you in a constant state of health, wealth, love and perfect self-expression.

lacking finances, and if this is a stable situation that has persisted for some time, then it's likely that most of the energetic signals you're exposing yourself to, are also vibrating at a similar frequency of financial lack. This includes the place where you live, the people you interact with, your work environment, events on your calendar, your furniture, your pots and pans and so on. Your being is immersed in a field of these signals, and this encourages you to vibrate at the same level.

If you continue to surround yourself with signals that reinforce your current state, then that state will persist indefinitely. You may be able to get away from it for a while, but you'll keep coming back to it if that's your equilibrium. Notice how your new vibrational frequency feels, not just emotionally but energetically. Then return to your old state of mind and frequency, and notice the vibrational difference between the two states.

For example, here's how I'd describe the vibration of being broke and deep in debt, a frequency many people transmit all the time: tight, knotted, chaotic, rough, dark grey, bitter, fast, and squeezed. Here's how I'd describe the vibration of financial abundance: open, free, clear, warm, sweet, green, flowing, smooth, bright, focused, and intense. Each vibration has a different energy signature. If you temporarily shift your default vibration to a state of financial lack just by imagining it as real, you will feel your energy shifting its frequency too. If you held that vibration long enough, you'd soon find that your physical reality followed suit.

If you want to raise your vibration, it's not a good idea to consistently expose yourself to incompatible lower frequency signals. If you watch the news and constantly see and hear about the financial crisis, recession, etc., notice what happens to your vibration. Then notice what happens to your finances in the long run. If you want to experience financial abundance, then stop watching mainstream news and try to avoid reading newspapers. This is the perfect time to read inspirational books or articles from financially successful individuals.

Time is not linear. Your mental state changes your perception of time. If you are unhappy or bored, time slows down. If you are afraid, time seems to stand still. When you feel happy, excited, and interested, time seems to speed by. The lower your frequency, the slower your perception of time. People engaged in high-vibration activities find that time passes quickly.

Overview

Learning to sense and control the vibrational frequencies you're emitting is very powerful. Once you master this, you can intentionally shift your frequency at will to experience what you desire. Even if it is just for fun! If you want to experience wealth, a new relationship, high energy, and good health, you can create that. It takes practice to adjust your vibrational

frequency correctly, so be patient with yourself. Your will is also a very important and powerful ingredient to manifesting everything. Focus your will and create what you see in your mind. Your limits are only what you can imagine and your creations are only as strong as your will. Will makes you take action. Fear is the enemy of will and makes you weak. Fear makes your creations feeble. There are also certain beings that feed on your fear. It is their sustenance.

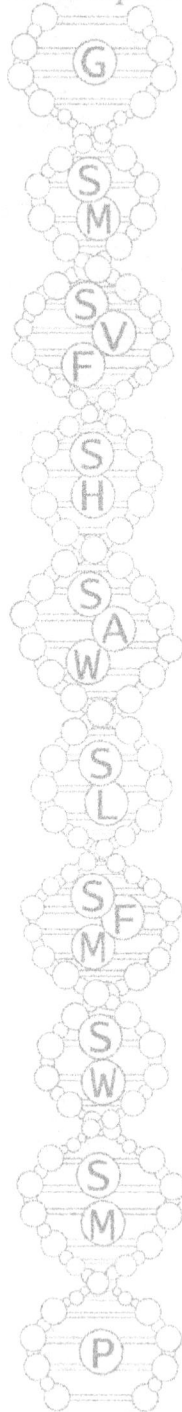

Chapter 4
Success in Health

The Blueprint

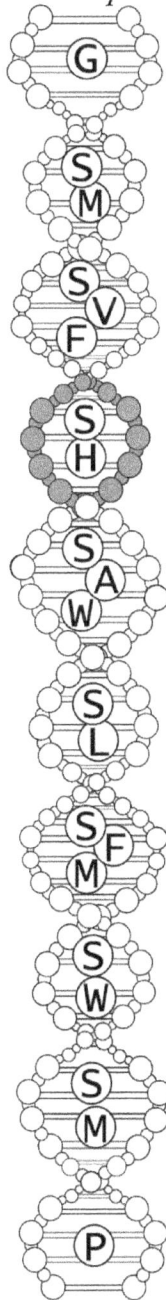

The Blueprint

The higher your vibrational frequency, the healthier and happier you are. Disease cannot exist in high frequency because it would not be energetically compatible with the high vibrating frequency of a healthy person. All illness has a vibrational component. Everything begins as a thought and as a feeling. This results in a specific vibration. Illness in the physical body is the effect of your thoughts and emotions, which are the cause. Happy people are typically healthy people.

Healthy Mind Healthy Body

In order to understand the basics of vibrational frequencies, let's look at a ceiling fan with paddles. If you turn on this fan to a slow setting, you can see the paddles moving in a circular motion and you can clearly see each individual paddle. Now turn the fan to a medium setting and you will see the paddles rotating faster but you can still make out each individual paddle. Now turn the fan to the highest setting. What you'll see is movement but you will not be able to make out each individual paddle. You also will not be able to see the electromagnetic energy around it, but it is there and it is quite powerful.

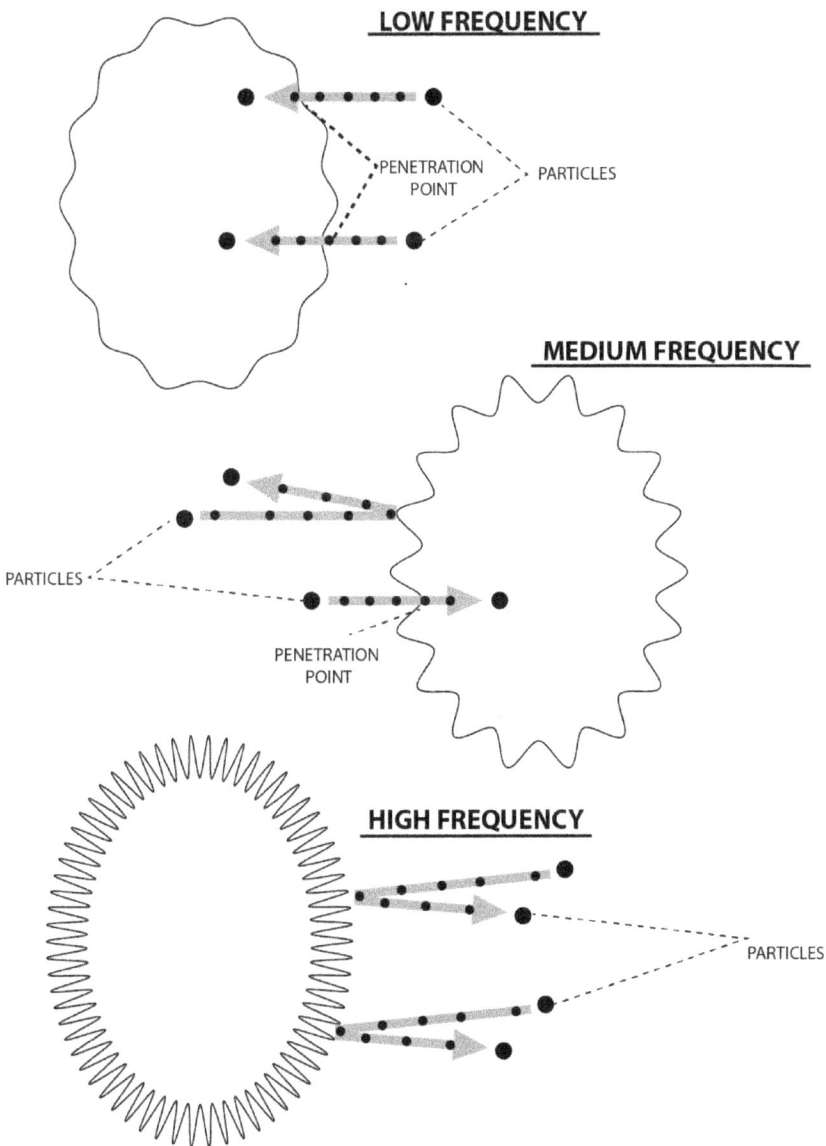

LOW FREQUENCY

PENETRATION POINT

PARTICLES

MEDIUM FREQUENCY

PARTICLES

PENETRATION POINT

HIGH FREQUENCY

PARTICLES

The higher your vibrational frequency is, the healthier and happier you are. Disease, bacteria, virus, negative energy, parasitic entities and other unwanted energies cannot exist in high frequency, because it is not energetically compatible with the high vibrating frequency of a healthy person.

Now imagine throwing a tiny ball at the fan. If it's on a slow setting, the ball has plenty of entry points and it will enter a space in between the paddles, and most likely will break the fan. If your fan is on a medium setting, the ball has less entry points but there is room for penetration. If your fan is on high or the highest setting, the ball will simply bounce off, as it will not be able to locate an entry point. This is how it works with disease, bacteria, virus, negative energy, and other unwanted energies. Furthermore, the higher your vibrational frequency the stronger the electromagnetic field around you.

There are various methods to measure your vibrational frequency. However, I think your life is the best measuring method of them all. If you are healthy, wealthy, happy, and fulfilled, and love yourself and most of the people in your life, it's safe to assume that you're vibrating at a high frequency. If you're ill, depressed, unhappy, angry, anxious, and suffering financially, it's because you're vibrating on a low frequency. You create absolutely everything in your life. This includes health and wellness.

The Fountain of Youth and Wellness

In creation, everything mirrors everything else. Just like galaxies, stars and human beings are constantly being recycled, so are the cells in your body. Some cells die and new ones are born, and this process continues as long as the physical bodies are alive. Nothing ever dies, everything simply transforms into different states of energy. Your physical body is designed to last much longer than what we typically see today. We are all familiar with the process of regeneration. If you cut your finger or get a bruise, in a few days it is healed. If you have surgery or even break a bone, depending on your frequency and state of health, sooner or later it heals. In the same fashion, our bodies are designed and created with a built-in self-healing mechanism for complete regeneration.

Technically your body is always new and has the potential to be perfectly healthy. Each organ in your body renews itself after a few days or weeks. For example, it takes six weeks for each cell of your liver to "die" and be replaced with all new cells. So every six weeks you have a new liver. The cells in your eyes regenerate every two days, which means that you have new eyes every two days. Your skin cells regenerate every twenty to thirty days, and your stomach lining regenerates every four days or so. You are always new.

If we are always new why then, with new cells and renewed organs do the old physical ailments and illnesses continue to show up even in the new blueprint? Why does an eye-problem not cure itself by the third or fourth day? The answer is: cellular memory. The memory from old cells, sometimes called a "phantom memory," is passed on to the new cells being born, so the eye problem is replicated time and time again, even though the cells are entirely new. This continues indefinitely until the cell memory programming is interrupted.

In order to interrupt the negative programming, and reprogram the cells towards health, you must raise your vibrational frequency!

The same applies for humanity. The collective cellular memory programming for human beings will continue until it's interrupted. The way to do that is to raise the frequency of the collective consciousness. Aging is a learned behavior and has become a meme or an agreement that human beings subscribe to. You simply agree to age. You are further programmed by the commercials you see on television and in magazines about aging and anti-aging. Even online you're constantly being bombarded with all kinds of mind programming ads and commercials. Dying is an agreement and a learned behavior as well. You are taught to die. Death is actually a transformation from one form of energy into another. You can tap into your own inner life force and fountain of youth at will. You must simply learn how to turn it on.

Emotional frequencies affect the natural laws or universal mechanics. Low frequencies keep you in a dense and slow energetic state, which makes you lazy, lethargic and unproductive. If you're vibrating at this low level, your immune system is weak and you are prone to illness. When you're vibrating at the highest frequency, you are luminescent and glowing from the inside out. It is a beautiful sight.

It's easy to spot someone who is vibrating on a low frequency. They are energetically heavy and usually it is difficult for those vibrating on higher frequencies to be around them, because they drain your energy. They also drain energy from everything and everyone around them, including earth. If you are currently one of those people, there are several great techniques to raise your frequency instantly and also for long term. You must raise your vibration before you are able to significantly improve your health. High frequency is very powerful and one person vibrating on a very high frequency counterbalances hundreds of thousands if not millions of individuals who calibrate very low.

Choose Health and Wellness

Being healthy, like everything else is a choice. In the infinite field of probabilities you already exist as both a healthy person and a sick one. You choose which physical reality you are in. Focus with gratitude on what is right about your health. Visualize your good health now, and the additional good health you choose. Do not focus or think about what's wrong because what you feed grows. For example, if you want to eliminate pain, don't think about how the pain hurts and how you want relief. Instead, think about the joy of being able to move freely and easily.

Remember if you don't give something your attention, it ceases to exist in your universe. In case of illness, you can visualize the good cells in your perfect immune system conquering all the bad cells. You can see the bad cells disappear one by one until they are all gone! The universe will bring you more of what you are paying attention to, whether it is pain, misery, health or happiness.

My constant state of mind and attitude is: "I am grateful for having excellent health, abundance of wealth, love, happiness and perfect self-expression." I also say it out loud several times per day. Use this or a similar statement to take your attention away from your pain or illness, and instead refocus on being grateful for the positive things in your life. Once you begin to broadcast positive energy, the universe will bring you more positive things for you to be grateful for. *Remember to tune in to yourself frequently and monitor your frequency.* If your frequency drops significantly and for a long period of time, you become susceptible to everything from the common cold to major illnesses. By the same token, if you raise your vibrational frequency, those ailments that you currently may have will disappear.

Nutrition and Vibration

The food you consume is the fuel that powers your body so that your body can transport you through this lifetime. Would you put bad gas or sand into the gas tank of your car? Of course not, because it would damage your car and you would have no transportation. Yet think about the fuel that you're putting inside your body. This fuel will determine to a great degree the life of your body along with the quality of life.

Today many people eat predominantly processed or dead food, which has virtually no life force and little or no nutritional value. This dead food has so many toxic ingredients, that it is guaranteed to make your body break down and eventually die. I suggest following this simple rule. If it's alive or recently has been, then you can eat it. If it comes in a can or a box, don't even consider it. All soda is terrible and many juices from concentrate are too. Spring or bottled water and freshly squeezed juice are your best choices. Overeating is another concern. Portions are getting bigger and people are consuming much more food than their bodies actually require. Your body has to work that much harder and use more energy to process the extra food and if it's not converted into energy, it of course, turns to extra fat. Moderation and balance are the answer.

Unless you have your own garden, it is difficult to find food that contains all the nutrients that a body needs. Supplements are often required. I suggest high vibration, nanotechnology vitamins and minerals. The average supplement is made up of larger particles and does not get absorbed by the body. Whereas, nanotechnology supplements are comprised of much smaller particles and are easily absorbed into the bloodstream. Human bodies, like planet earth are comprised of 70% water. Water is a conductor for electricity. Our bodies are electromagnetic in nature and water is vital to the health and longevity of our bodies. Are you giving your body enough water? If your car runs out of water, it starts to burn and you can't drive. Your body operates in a very similar way. No water, no power. All systems will eventually fail.

Lifestyle Choices and Frequency

Lifestyle choices affect your frequency. Stress will lower your frequency significantly, as will anger, jealousy, greed and fear. Exposure to negative energy from people, places, toxins in food, and household items will also lower your frequency. Certain electromagnetic energies, such as the ones from cellular phones and computers can interfere with and scramble your frequency. Drugs, both street and prescription are the single most poisonous substance which will not only drop your frequency, but will eventually kill the body. Sex with people who vibrate on very low frequencies will lower yours. Obviously the choice is always up to you.

Healthy Vibration

There are some great activities that can help to raise vibration: meditation, yoga, exercise, hiking, swimming, great sex with a high vibrating individual that you are bonded with, getting a massage, or taking a walk in nature barefoot. I highly recommend swimming in the ocean, hiking in the mountains, walking or jogging in the park, or just relaxing by a lake. These outdoor activities will not only help you tune into the high frequency of universal love, but also activate your physical body, which will make you feel more "alive." It is also vital to your overall health to keep your intestines clean. Many people have waste sitting in their intestines for years without realizing it, which begins to rot and the resulting toxins will affect the entire body. A good natural, herbal nightly cleanse will keep you healthy and glowing.

Love is a high frequency energy, which keeps your body clear and flowing. Fall in love as often as you can. Most importantly fall in love with yourself. For example, I'm having a life-long love affair with myself. We love each other and always get along. When you love yourself, fear will not exist in your universe. Fear is a very low frequency and will create a wall or barrier between you and all positive energy, which blocks healing. Healing occurs when high-frequency energy flows through the body, transmuting the negative, stale and toxic energy, which caused the illness in the first place.

Auto Correct Healing

Our physical bodies come equipped with a brilliant self-healing mechanism. Once we raise our vibrational frequency and get out of our own way, the body can and does fix itself. You just have to change your attitude. When the sick person genuinely forgives himself and the person who he thinks caused the ill feelings of resentment, hate, fear, or other negative emotion, the negative energy block breaks down and disappears. Nature in general is a great purifier. Fire, water, earth, and air are magical. Walking barefoot on earth or on grass allows you to reconnect with the earth and your negative energies will be drained through your feet and transmuted. A breeze or wind will clear your energy quickly. Swimming, especially in the ocean is very beneficial as is a hot bath with sea salt. Fire is the most powerful purification of all. Burning old photographs, letters, and objects that may be associated with the old negative emotions transmutes the negativity of repressed memories and changes the energy around you.

It is fairly easy to feel if your vibration has dropped. You begin to see everything and everyone around you in a negative light and you get cranky and irritable. Since like attracts like, only people with similar frequencies will feel comfortable in your presence. All addictions are behaviors, which we repeat in order to suppress natural feelings. These may be over-eating, compulsive spending, drinking too much alcohol, drug abuse, or any number of negative behaviors. When you feel your frequency drop, raise your vibrational frequency, and you'll be as good as new, or better.

A Quick Pick-Me-Up: works in 60 seconds.

• Get up and move around or jump up and down
• Take a brisk walk or go for a swim.
• Twirl, jog in place or dance.
• Listen to your favorite happy song.

This will revive and raise your frequency immediately because when you get up and physically move, it will get your circulation going which in turn will shift your frequency. Music is a frequency as well and is just as effective for short term and long term shift.

Overview

Everything in life is a choice, including your health. Your state of mind influences your choices and your physical body and physical reality manifests those choices. You now have the ability to clearly see how to make adjustments to your lifestyle and the wisdom to make better choices. Choose health and happiness because that is your birthright and have faith in yourself. A phrase, an image or a passage from a book could be your trigger and your life will change in an instant.

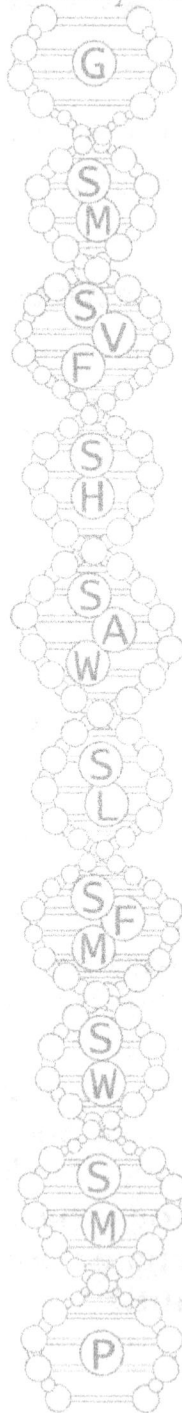

The Blueprint

Chapter 5
Success in Wealth

The Blueprint

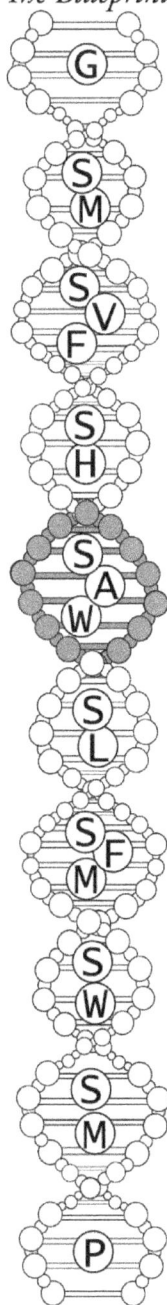

The Blueprint

Success is a state of mind, and it's a choice and a feeling. Wealth is a choice, and so is poverty. You may think that there is no way, anyone in their right mind would choose poverty. Well, I didn't say that they were in their right mind or that they made that choice consciously. In fact, the choice of poverty, fear, anger, misery, and illness is always made unconsciously and by default.

Success and wealth go hand-in-hand. They are twins. Everything is a frequency and you resonate with those people and conditions that match your own frequency. What you emanate and broadcast, you attract and pick up. From this day forward pay attention to your vibrational pattern and be aware of what you are broadcasting. Focus on transmitting the energy of success and abundance, and your physical universe will reflect that back to you. This is the only way success becomes consistent and permanent in every area of your life. Think of it like programming. You are the programmer of yourself and your life. You adjust your frequency and program your universe to bring into it what you choose.

Success and Affluence

The best way I can describe my approach to success is that it is a way of life. It is a carefully constructed, deliberate and consistent strategy, which governs my thoughts and emotions. I control my thoughts and emotions. They do not control me. I can choose to be stern with someone for an hour in order to perhaps reprimand and teach them a lesson, but then I quickly jump out of it because if I were to vibrate on that frequency for a long time, it would be damaging to my universe. I make choices based on the ultimate end result I am trying to bring about. I can win or lose at will, depending on what is convenient for me at that particular time. Ultimately, I Always Win!

Success is not about a particular accomplishment or win. It's not even about a series of achievements. If you focus on one specific goal, which you designate as your success, there is a brief period of exhilaration or a high, which you may ride for a short while. Then you have to designate a new goal and you will be right back on the level of effort, trying to get there in order to feel that high again. If you climb to the top of Mt. Everest, do you really want to go back down and start all over again? I think not!

Thus, you find yourself on an emotional roller coaster and your life becomes a series of ups and downs, with frequencies reflecting that. If that is your way of life, you energetically attract to yourself more ups and downs leading you to ride a perpetual emotional and energetic roller coaster. This roller coaster leads to stress, frustration, and self-doubt.

Try it my way you just might like it! Based on The Blueprint, abundant success is about flowing along with life, aligning your frequency harmoniously with that of what you want, taking advantage of the universal mechanics, and enjoying the journey. True success is a constant sense of inner satisfaction and fulfillment and most importantly, self-love.

Lana's Way

I am successful every day in every way. I know this to be true therefore it is true. It is a meme, which I intentionally created and by paying attention to it, I keep it in place and in my physical reality. I wake up in the morning, go through my day, and go to sleep at night with the same consistent knowledge and feeling. It is the energy I broadcast constantly, even in my sleep. This manifests in my physical reality. I believe the following:

I am alive. I am healthy. I am wealthy. I am powerful. I am generous. I love and I am loved. I am gracious. I am kind. I am beautiful. I am brilliant. I am wise. I am G.O.D. What do you currently believe about yourself? Think about it and write it down.

_____

_____

_____

_____

_____

_____

_____

_____

_____

_____

My physical reality reflects what I believe and know to be true. If you look at what you have written down, you will find that yours does too. Now think about what you want to be without any limitations whatsoever and write that down:

_____

_____

_____

_____

_____

_____

_____

_____

_____

_____

Now imagine and feel what it would feel like if you were all those things that you just wrote down. Remember that feeling. Read what you wrote in the wanted section to yourself or out loud three times per day for 30 days and then spend a few moments feeling that same emotion again. This is the fastest and most effective way to raise your frequency and attract what you choose to yourself. The key is to be consistent with it and even after you achieve the desired results, to continue using this system because you want this to be a way of life. Once you get it, you have to hold on to it.

Abundance in general is so much that your cup is overflowing. It is more than you can use. If you have more than you can use then you can afford to be generous with others. It is really for the greatest good of the greatest number for you to have an abundance of wealth. Abundance of wealth is also a frequency. Although it is challenging to depict this frequency on paper, this is pretty close.

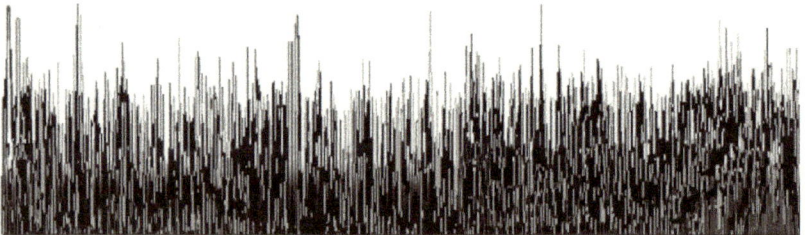

This is a very high frequency of consistent abundance of wealth. In order to maintain a life of abundance, this is the frequency you must live in.

Money is energy just like everything else in the cosmos, and at its basic form is light, G.O.D particles. Based on the design of The Blueprint, the flow of abundance is always aimed right at you. It is aimed at everyone. However, your beliefs, thoughts and feelings, create a blockade or barrier around you. So this flow goes around to you or to someone else who is open to receiving it. It is up to you to remove the beliefs or memes, which block your in-flow of abundance and instead focus your attention on being clean, clear, and open to receiving the flow of abundance. All you have to do is choose abundance. Remember everything already exists in the infinite field, including a wealthy you. All you have to do is choose that one and it will become real in your physical world.

If you believe either consciously or subconsciously that money is hard to get, the energy you broadcast will harmonize with compatible energy in waveforms, transmuting it into particles. Then these particles, like tiny magnets, will attract additional matching particles and will form matter. Your physical reality will reflect to you that money is hard to get. On the other hand, if you believe that you always have money, it's easy to get and the flow of abundance is constantly aimed at you, and you are open to and grateful for receiving it, your life will reflect that back to you. You will have money coming at you from different sources all the time and your affluent lifestyle will be permanent.

You are literally programming your life. This is one of the ways I program my life. I refuse to believe what others believe. Their world is not mine. I create my own reality, consciously and intentionally. I broadcast out into the universe what I am and what I am not, available for. I never subscribe to someone else's reality because I don't

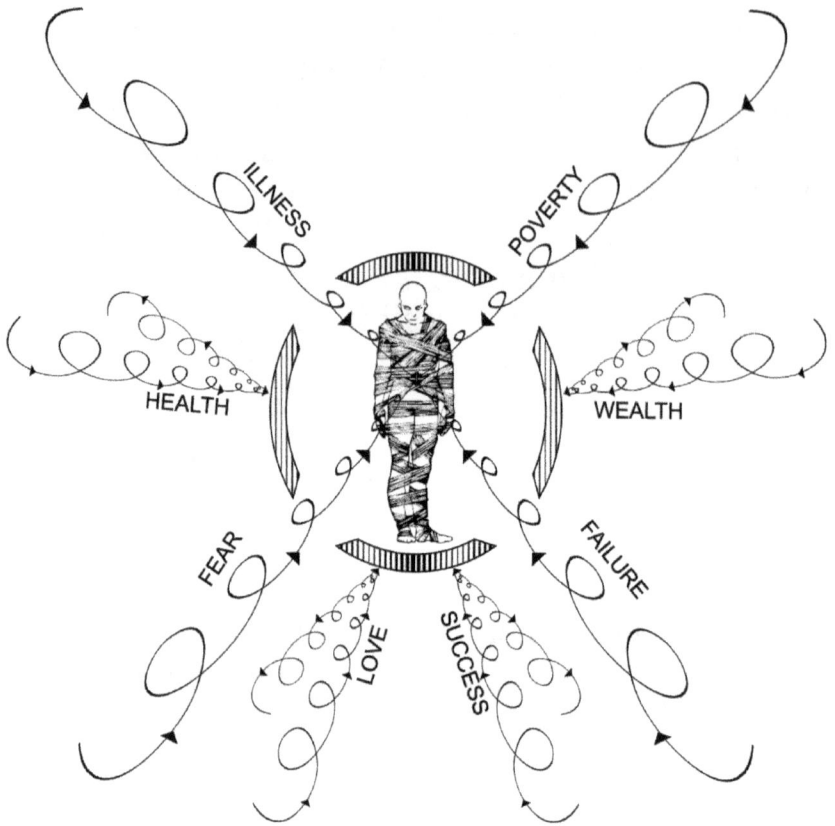

This person is bound by memes, lives in fear and vibrates on a very low frequency. He is unconsciously attracting to himself illness, failure, poverty and fear. He cannot consciously make any changes to his universe unless he cuts many of his memes and raises his frequency. His existing memes and low frequency block the inflow of health, wealth, love and success. This is a permanent state of existence for the vast majority of human beings today.

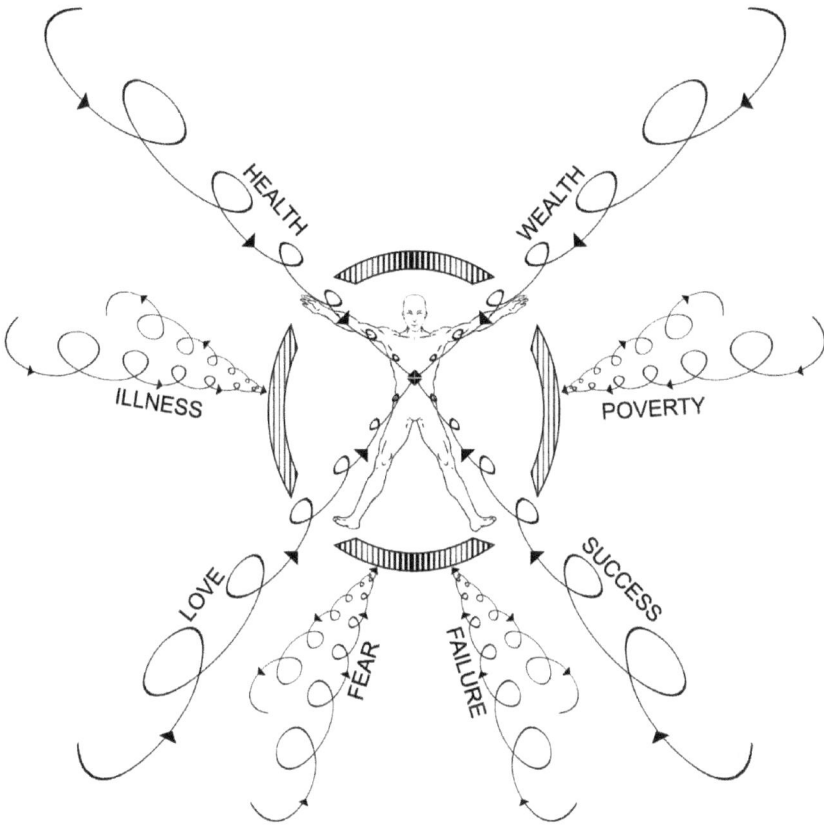

This is Lana. I am completely free because I am not bound by negative memes and I vibrate on an extremely high frequency. I live in a constant state of perfect health, abundance of wealth, love and perfect self-expression. I am consciously open to receiving the inflow of the same harmonious frequencies and intentionally create whatever I choose. I am therefore blocked and protected from the inflow of low vibrating frequencies of illness, poverty, failure and fear. I manage and control my thoughts and emotions, only paying attention to what I choose to have in my universe. The undersireable energy bounces away from me and flows to others who are open and available to it. This is my successful state of mind. Strive to create your successful state of mind so you too can have it all.

like it. I like my reality.

I am not available for illness, poverty, fear, stress, anxiety, and the rest of the negative energies out there. I don't ever think about them nor do I give them any attention whatsoever. Therefore, they go around me to those who are available for it, and that is pretty much 99.9% of the population of this planet. What I am available for is permanent success in everything, abundance of wealth, perfect health, love, grace and perfect self-expression. Since I am open to receiving these energies and they are already aimed at me anyway, they come straight for me and I accept them gratefully with open arms and chakras.

Look at how you look at things and examine your memes, which are agreements that you believe to be true or real. You may have been told that thinking about money is bad and you may feel guilty even thinking about money. You may have been raised to believe that money is the root of all evil. You may think that you're not worthy for one reason or another and don't deserve to have money. You may think that only people with the highest level of education get rich and if you don't have this education, then you'll never be rich. If you believe either consciously or subconsciously any of these things, then your life will play out accordingly.

There are countless possible money related memes that may have been in place since childhood, and are now affecting your thought process and can be blocking your flow of abundance. Religion typically creates negative money memes and people begin to consciously and subconsciously block their flow of money. I find this fascinating especially since religion seems to be the most profitable and recession proof business since antiquity.

Get rid of those memes that are standing in the way of what you want. If you want to be rich, then you are entitled to be rich simply because you want it! Some people are happy being poor and living in a monastery or sitting on top of a mountain and meditating all day. Wonderful! Some people are happy being extraordinarily wealthy, with beautiful homes, exotic cars, and private jets and yachts. Fabulous! One is not better or worse than the other. It is a personal choice. If being wealthy will make you happy then you should be wealthy.

You Owe It to Yourself and
The Universe to be Rich

Money has been mistreated, misunderstood, and abused for thousands of years. Money is actually spiritual and beautiful. The currency of money is like electricity. You can use electricity to light your home or you can use it to electrocute, hurt, or kill people. That doesn't make electricity bad. It's your choice how you use it. The same goes for money. You can use it with ethics, integrity and honor to have a great quality of life. On the other hand you can use money to belittle, harm, or kill people. That is abuse of money. If you continue to abuse money, you will eventually lose it.

Regardless of your current financial status, there is nothing wrong with wanting more money, exotic cars, beautiful homes, gorgeous jewelry, designer clothing, glamorous vacations, or whatever else you're dreaming about. If anyone tells you otherwise, banish them immediately. You don't need anyone's permission or approval to get the amazing life you want and deserve.

It is in everyone's best interest for you to be rich. The more money you have, the more money you spend. The more money you spend, the more you add to the economy. The more you add to the economy, the more it benefits your city, state, and country. You owe it to yourself and to your country to be extremely rich.

Let's Get Money!

Money is made up of the exact same building blocks as you and I, and everything else. It is G.O.D particles vibrating on a specific frequency. Money is energy. Once you adjust your frequency to that of abundance, you will be attracting to yourself those vibrational patterns. There are several techniques that work like magic to get into the money mode.

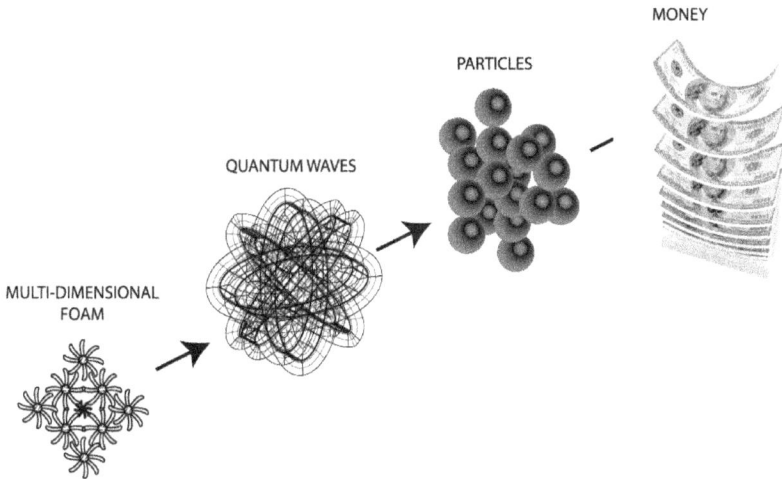

MONEY

PARTICLES

QUANTUM WAVES

MULTI-DIMENSIONAL
FOAM

When you begin to broadcast the thoughts and emotions of abundance of wealth, regardless if you currently have this wealth in your physical universe, the energy you send out will transform waveforms and multi-dimensional foam into particles, which will then attract other matching particles and will create physical matter in your life. Money is made up of the same G.O.D particles as everything else, including you and me. This is how you create money and wealth.

1. **Fast Money:** Need some money quickly? Get some cash, real money, or play money; dollar bills are perfect. Hold it with both hands, look at it, smell it and feel its energy. Focus on how good it feels to have this money and be grateful for having it. Visualize yourself as a living money magnet and money is coming at you from every direction and you are open to receiving it. The money you're holding in your hands is attracting to itself more money. Money

71

is attracted to money, and even if you're holding play money at the moment it is still attracting real money because you're visualizing it as real money. With this quick and simple technique, you have just shifted your frequency to that of getting money. * Note: Never say, "I need" or "I want" instead say, "I choose!"

2. **Long Money:** Can you imagine yourself being a millionaire right now? If you can, then do so. Don't worry if you can't because it could be a challenge to feel like a millionaire if you've never been one. Can you imagine yourself $1,000 richer? $10,000 richer? $100,000 richer? Stop where you can really feel it. Work with that feeling of being richer for a while. The more you work with it, the easier it becomes to believe it. The more you believe it, the more your subconscious will direct you to make it happen. It may be small things at first like getting refunds or gifts and credit, or fewer bills, but the more you do it, the bigger the prize. Be grateful for all of them no matter how big or small. Do this 15 to 30 minutes per day every day and watch the money flow right to you.

3. **Visions of Money:** I love doing vision boards and have done them since I was a child. Take a picture of yourself and put it in the middle of the board. Then get actual money or play money or pictures of money, along with wealth related headlines from magazines and newspapers and

glue them to your board around yourself. Keep this board in a prominent place where you can see it all the time. Every day or every week add more pictures of wealth, money, exotic cars, mansions, or whatever it is that you want to have. Now you are surrounded by wealth and energetically starting to attract it into your physical life.

4. **I Want It All and I Want It Now!** This is the fastest and most effective way to change your life! You must intentionally disconnect from as many energetic patterns you are currently compatible with, whether it is poverty or mediocrity, or wherever you may be at the moment. You must then intentionally connect with the energy patterns of abundance of wealth by changing the dominant frequency you're broadcasting. This means you must change completely as much in your life as possible. You are both a transmitter and receiver of energy and since you're constantly receiving energy from your environment, you have to change it. It's not as difficult as it sounds but it does require courage and willpower. You have to want it!

   Banish all the losers in your life. This includes people you're dating. If they are going nowhere and are weighing you down, cut them loose. Surround yourself with ambitious, rich, and successful people. Just being in their frequency will help shift yours. If you don't currently have people like this, no problem.

Start reading books and watching movies about successful, rich people. Get inspired. Don't watch, read, or listen to anything that is contrary to what you want.

It may feel uncomfortable at first, but eventually you'll start to integrate this new energy and your own vibrational pattern will soon adjust and harmonize with the new frequency in your life. Get into this feeling of abundance on a daily basis. Have fun with this and remember you are designing your new and exciting life! The only limits are self-imposed. Be brave and daring. Go for your dreams.

Most people focus their attention on what they don't want and what they fear and in doing so create their lives. Some people are born into poverty and all their friends and family are poor, and they both transmit and receive this energy constantly. They continue to see themselves as poor people so they live in poverty and desperation until they die. Others are in debt and see themselves as people who owe money to other people. They struggle to make their ends meet and their lives are spent struggling.

How do you break the cycle and change your life? The key is imagination. You must think, feel, and perceive differently in order to get something different. The universe responds to your emotional body. It all starts with a vision of you being in a different life. If you believe and feel that you are a money magnet you will become one. If you currently have bills and debts, don't focus on them. I am not telling you to ignore them. Set up a debt repayment system to get them off your mind for now, and then get back to focusing on abundance. It usually takes 30 days to reprogram anything. However, you could start seeing results immediately. Most people do. This worked for me and it will work for you.

Overview

Your current financial state is not as important as how you feel. If you don't feel rich, you will always be poor. There are millionaires who complain about their bills, taxes, and investments and they still have money worries. Then, there are people who live on a modest income, but always seem to have enough money to do the things that they enjoy. It's important to feel rich. You don't have to wait to have lots of cash in your pocket to start feeling rich and abundant right now. Your emotions are like muscles. The more you feel an emotion, the easier it is to feel that emotion again. Just like muscles, if you don't use certain emotions, you lose them. The choice is always yours. The universal mechanism is triggered by your emotions and their intensity.

Continuous success and wealth is the effect of your perceptions and feelings. If

you see, feel and expect yourself to be wealthy and successful, you will be. This blueprint and mechanism should become a permanent way of life. Nutrition experts tell you not to go on a diet, and instead they suggest you change your eating habits. This same theory applies to abundance of wealth. Stop being on a financial starvation diet and change your money related thoughts, feelings and perceptions, and start enjoying the decadent wealthy lifestyle you deserve. You deserve it because you want it!

Chapter 6
Success in Love
The Blueprint

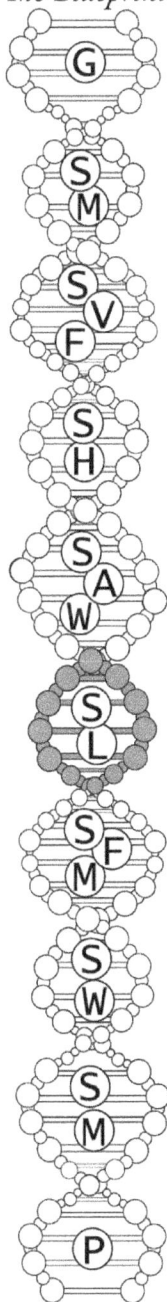

The Blueprint

Love makes the world go around. Everyone talks about love and everyone wants to be in love. Everyone wants to love and be loved, but what is love really? Love is more than a feeling and a concept. Love is a frequency and it's vital to all life. Life built on love is a life of magic and beauty. There has to be at least one person in your life that you truly love and at least one that loves you. It could be a parent, sibling, child, your spouse or yourself. Love is that delicious feeling of warmth, coherence, safety, security and belonging. That's the frequency of love. When you learn to truly love yourself, you feel that emotion and that frequency all the time. If you vibrate on love, you can tune into the living library of earth and instantly connect with all of life and access information about anything and everything. When the choices you make in life come from the wisdom that you absorb from this living library, you can truly create your very own heaven on earth!

What is Love?

The actual energy or frequency of love is something that most people don't understand. If you don't know what it feels like you may not know what you are looking for. Let's look at the actual frequency of love. In our universe, particles or matter flows outward from the middle. The energy of excitement and happiness is constantly streaming into our universe from the center and keeps the matter contained in our universe. Love and security is the stabilizing coherent energy that presses inward from the outer G.O.D consciousness blanket. This energy is warming, comforting and holds us in. It feels like a never-ending full body hug. That is what G.O.D's love is and since we are all G.O.D we can transmit and receive this energy from one another, our universe, and the cosmos at large.

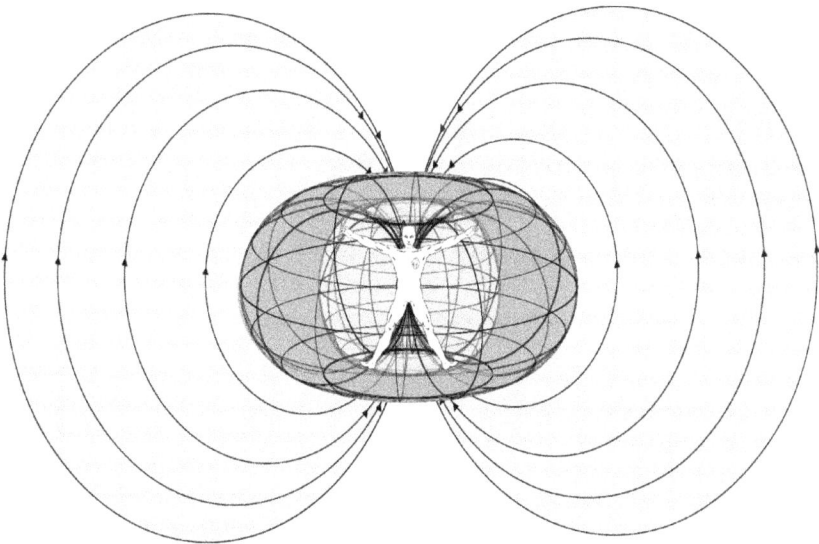

The electromagnetic field of love sustains our universe and holds it in place. We are surrounded by love all the time. The vast majority of people vibrate on the frequency of fear and thus, are incompatible with the frequency of love. All you have to do is rise to the energy of love and connect with the cosmic energy and watch your physical life transform instantly.

The frequency of love is G.O.D particles vibrating at its original authentic frequency, and it is the same energy that makes up every living being in the cosmos, including us. When you realize that we are all one and you live in harmony with all creation, you experience the feeling and frequency of love. Everything begins with love for self. When you begin to truly love yourself, everything changes instantaneously. When you broadcast your love for yourself, you will energetically attract others who love you too. Then in the blink of an eye, you notice that everyone and everything in the universe loves you. Money loves you. The world loves you. By the same token whoever or whatever does not love you is no longer able to enter your vibrational field and is simply not a part of your universe. This is the ultimate way to banish your haters by the way. Haters operate on a very low frequency of fear so even if they want to come close, they can't. It is a natural hater repellent. Let's do this fun exercise. What do you love about yourself? Write it down.

_____

_____

_____

_____

_____

_____

_____

_____

_____

_____

Every day find something new to love about yourself and add it to this list. I am hoping that you will need a lot more room than the few lines you have here.

_____

_____

_____

_____

_____

_____

_____

_____

_____

_____

Unity and coherence is the mechanism behind the frequency of love. G.O.D particles collect their organizing patterns and the universal mechanics from the information from the cosmos, which is constantly flowing into and throughout the universe. This phenomenon ensures the compatibility and integrity of the universal patterns and laws of the cosmic blueprint. What we call love is the feeling experience of understanding and unity coming together. In order for physical life to remain intact, related G.O.D particles must share information with one another and they need to love one another in order to join forces and work towards a common goal based on their purpose. From particles to atoms and cells, all energy arranges itself and clings together through the sharing of information and love for the greatest good of their organisms. Human beings unite and work together for their families. Families and societies are organized in exactly the same way for the greater good of our organism, the human race. The human race must unite and work together for the greatest good of our planet and all of creation through the sharing of relevant information and shared meme chords and love.

Love is Life

The cosmos is alive and vibrating with information and organizational principles. G.O.D consciousness wraps around the world of space and time, directing organization into our universe, and it is this inward flowing force that we call love. Since you now know that you are G.O.D and the master of the galaxy that is you, and the trillions of G.O.D particles that live in your galaxy that keep you together, how could you not love yourself and all those that are living within you? When you love yourself, you become in harmony with the frequency of love, and since like attracts like, you will naturally attract more of that which loves you.

Moreover, you will understand that everyone and everything around you is also G.O.D and how can you not love G.O.D or yourself? Since we are all comprised of the same G.O.D particles and are all a part of one vast and infinite G.O.D consciousness, then we are all ONE G.O.D We are all a part of one beautiful elephant. You are me and I am you. At this point in time it just so happens that the cells of the elephant's toe can't see the cells of the same elephant's ear, and they have no idea that they all make up one elephant. That is why people think they are alone and separated from everyone else. Separation is a mere illusion. We are all a part of one elephant and we must ensure that the whole elephant is healthy and is thriving in order for each individual cell to survive. If any part of the elephant breaks down, the whole elephant is destroyed.

I love myself because I know myself. I love my husband and my children because I know them. I also see them as G.O.D and miraculous parts of one infinite G.O.D consciousness, and we are all one. I think it is very difficult to truly love what you don't know or understand. You may love in a blind way, but it will be a conditional love based on whether the object of your love lives up to your expectations or perceptions, which may be distorted. I learned to love myself unconditionally and constantly. Love is life. Love is light. Love yourself first and foremost, and only then will you be able to love another. When you love yourself, it is projected out into the cosmos. The outside world is a mere reflection of the inner you. Therefore, people will mirror your self-love back to you and you will feel love in the air, literally. Life is simply reflecting back to you your own viewpoint and feelings about yourself. What's on the inside is always reflected on the outside.

Another benefit of love is that it repels hate and fear. Love is the highest vibrational frequency. Love is the frequency of light. Entities and beings vibrating on the frequency that is significantly lower like anger and fear are literally blinded by the light of love. They cannot come close or even look at it from too close a distance, or if they choose to come closer without looking, they will simply get burned. That means that they will be transmuted and returned back to the light or G.O.D. It is similar to the bugs that fly into the light boxes outside and you hear them being buzzed or zapped. We vibrate on various frequencies, which makes some beings shine brighter than others. The higher your frequency the more light you contain.

Some beings are actually repulsed by the light and some are attracted to it. For example, there are insects that are attracted to the light and there are others that are not. This phenomenon is known as phototaxes. Certain insects such as cockroaches or earthworms have negative phototaxis, meaning they are repelled by exposure to light. Moths, flies, and many other flying insects have positive phototaxis, meaning they are naturally attracted to it. Since everything in the cosmos is replicated, there are some people who are naturally attracted beings of light and want to be in the presence of these people. There are also those who are repulsed by beings of light, and those are negative phototaxis people. The negative ones are usually blinded by light and if they come too close, they'll get burned or zapped, kind of like insects in the insect catch light.

Love and Grace are
Two Sides of the Same Coin

Grace is divine mercy and compassion, and always accompanies love. It dissolves karma, creates miracles, and can change matter. We G.O.D particles have accepted the opportunity to be born on this planet in a physical body to learn about and to experience feelings and emotions. We are here to live not just to exist. We also have free will in order to create our own reality and our own unique life in a place where every thought, word, and deed manifests. As challenging as it may seem, in theory we should accept everyone and everything as they are, without judgment, which includes ourselves. On earth we experience duality, and dark and light energy, which comes from the free will. Duality is a learning experience to expand our light.

We all come from something else based on our evolutionary ancestry line. If you look around you'll notice that people kind of look like animals, reptiles, or insects. Some of us look like cats, others look like elephants, some like marsupials, and others look like spiders or a combination of several different animals and/or other living beings. There is no better or worse. We are just all different. We are all made of G.O.D particles, from worms to humans, and beings on other planets and in other existences. When Jesus said that God is everywhere that is what he meant. All of creation is made of G.O.D particles, including us. Every species of life that you see today survived because of love.

What's normal for me is not normal for you. What is normal for a worm is not normal for a moth. What is normal to a bunny is not normal for a bird. Human beings tend to judge one another based on their own subjective view of normal. That is as silly as an eagle judging a dog for not being able to fly. What is important is that we appreciate everyone for their unique nature and admire them and the G.O.D within them. Together we are a part of one consciousness currently residing on this planet.

We are all sharing this planet right now and should respect everyone's space. We are designed to join forces by looking for the commonality in each other. Just as you were invited to be here for this learning on earth, so are animals, insects, trees, and plants. All are learning and evolving. You are entitled to your space just as they are entitled to theirs. Everyone is entitled to their own territory. So, in theory, if you kill a bug, as silly as that might sound, you should talk to the higher consciousness of the bugs and remind them that they are in your territory and ask them to move. After two warnings if they don't, tell them that you'll have to return them to the light if they don't honor your space. If they are outside, then you just let them be because you have no right to kill them. They are in their own territory.

When you understand The Blueprint you begin to see life as the wondrous phenomenon that it is. You will learn to listen to your intuition and become the designer and creator of your own life. In our busy life, it's sometimes easy to forget this and it helps to slow down once in a while and reconnect with the true nature of creation and with our authentic selves. Love and Grace are two sides of the same coin. Through love and grace, we can transmute our karmic debts, change emotional feelings, heal relationships and the physical body. However we must be ready to receive it. We created all our situations consciously or unconsciously, and we must understand why we created them and what lessons we've learned from them. We created by default or by design every single aspect of our lives. We have no one to blame that includes ourselves. Once we realize that we are all creators and masters of our own fate, we realize that we have the power to change every aspect as well.

Overview

At the highest level of evolution, you simply know that it is what it is and stop judging. There is no need to forgive because there is nothing to forgive. You created everything in your universe. Everything is an experience and a learning process. Love and grace are two sides of the same coin. Love does not exist without grace. We can offer grace through our compassion, mercy, empathy, and love. What we send out is what we get back. Live in a divine manner and you will have a divine life. A change of attitude will change and heal your mind,

your body, and your life. Love is all around you all the time. Love, which is the foundation of all creation, is a remarkable orchestra, which is constantly playing the most beautiful cosmic symphony, and if you can only tune in and hear it, your life will never be the same again.

Chapter 7
Success of Freedom

The Blueprint

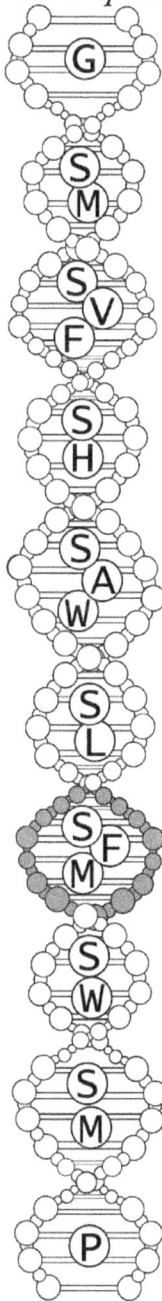

The Blueprint

We hold the power of creation within ourselves and we create our reality simply by choosing what we place our attention and focus on. Freedom is encoded into our DNA and is our birthright. We are all G.O.D so can you imagine G.O.D not having freedom? Sounds silly, doesn't it? Unfortunately instead of practicing, guarding, and protecting our freedom, we choose to give it away to anyone who will take it.

We are living in society with enough rules and regulations to make your head spin. We have a government that constantly passes new laws designed to suppress humanity further and punish them for practically walking the wrong way. This is all done, they say for our own good. Not quite, nevertheless this is not the subject of this book.

The society we live in is toxic. Our culture is becoming so institutionalized that people stop thinking for themselves and are now told what to think and when to do so. Freedom may seem like a nice but faraway dream or illusion. It may appear to be so on the surface but if we look deeper, we will find that everything is a choice. Our choice. We all have the right to manage our own frequencies.

A typical human being aka The Bio-Robot and modern day slave, who is programmed and bound by countless memes including addiction to electronics and drugs meme. He is a slave to religion and consumerism, and believes almost everything force-fed to him by the government, media and society in general. He is vibrating on the frequency of a slug or a worm.

Programming

Programming begins as early as birth. Children are often told that they are flawed, that they are born sinners, and that there is something wrong with them. They are compared to their siblings at home and criticized in school. Our entire educational system seems to be designed to turn all children into bio-robots who are taught to follow directions without questioning. If a child is free spirited or simply different, they are usually punished or diagnosed with A.D.D (Attention Deficit Disorder) or other 3-letter conditions or illnesses and then medicated into submission. Then they are bombarded by television, radio, internet, and video games with more negative information.

If that is not enough, we have religion. Most of the mainstream religions will tell you that you are a sinner, bad, and unworthy. They tell you that you must pray, repent for some ridiculous alleged sins, and follow the most bizarre and silly rules and regulations. Then they tell you that you should fear a scary, powerful, and maybe even a vengeful God. It's no wonder people grow up believing that they are powerless and spend their entire lives living in fear. It is also not surprising that people cannot think for themselves and that God, government, religious leaders, teachers, and everyone else knows what is better for them than they do. My favorite mind control mechanism is definitely, "I surrender to your will!" Brain Washing 101.

This is a very powerful and well-designed mind control mechanism put in place and enforced on our planet. It's a brilliant way to control the masses. Some people are beginning to understand that it is simply programming. Much like a computer program, your mind can be reprogrammed and cleaned up. It is time to wake up people! You were not born sinners and you are not subject to the wrath of God. You are creations of G.O.D and you are here to live a free and happy life so that you can experience and evolve. We are all G.O.D particles, vessels of light, and while some shine brighter than others, and some barely shine at all, the pilot light is lit in every single living being. The only differences are in the vibrational frequencies, the choices we make, the resulting karma, and the memes or agreements that we subscribe.

Memes

Memes are agreements that we believe to be true or real. We come into this lifetime with certain memes, both spiritually and through cellular memory, and we continue to form new ones all the time. Usually the memes we form or subscribe to as children affect us throughout our lives because unconsciously we make choices based on those memes without even realizing it. For example, if growing up your mother told you that dogs were dangerous you might grow up believing that it's true, and you might spend your entire adult life

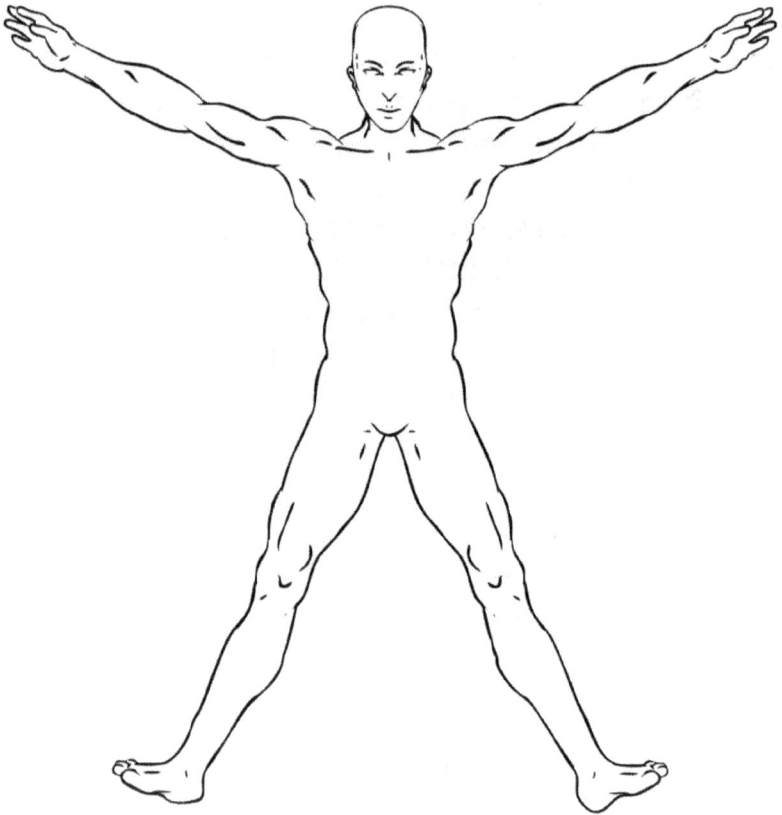

This picture represents Lana. I am free from negative memes and
therefore can fully express my individual viewpoint and create what I
choose when I choose to do it. This is the state of mind you want to
achieve. This is what life is all about.

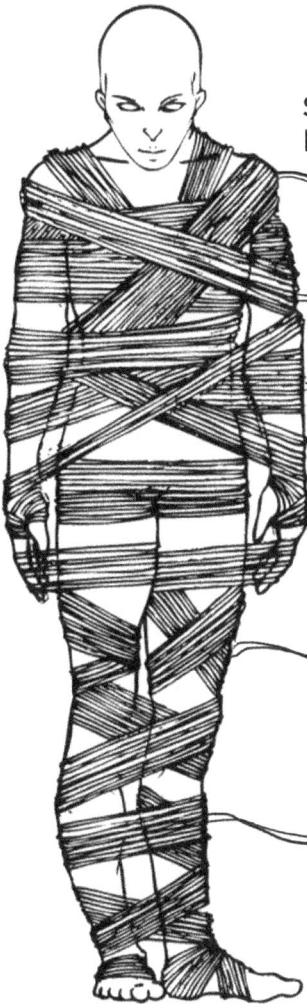

SEX BEFORE MARRIAGE
IS WRONG.

MUST FEAR GOD.

MEAT IS BAD FOR YOU.

I WILL NEVER GET OUT
OF MY CURRENT LIFE.

DRUGS HELP ME COPE
WITH EVERYDAY LIFE.

I MUST OWN MORE
MATERIAL THINGS.

This person is a representative of a typical modern human being who is so tightly bound by the negative memes, that he cannot freely think, move or create. This person does not live. Here merely exists and survives.

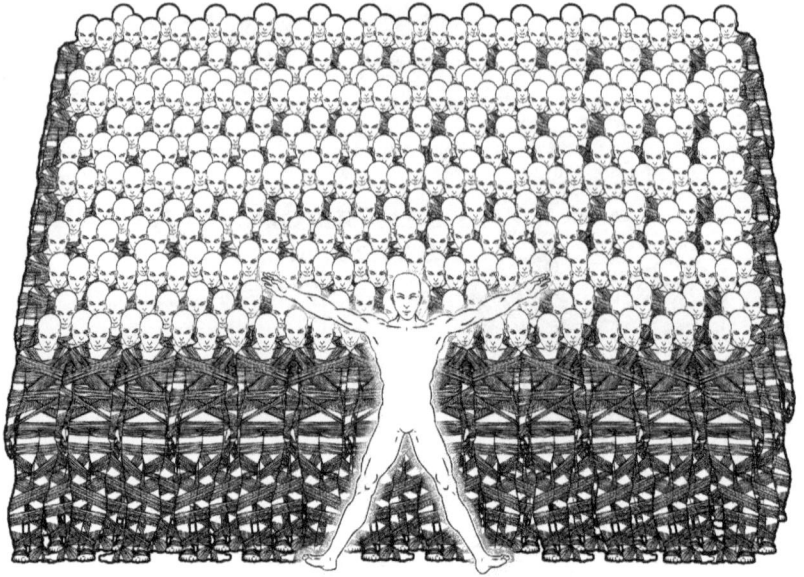

The figure infront is Lana. I am free from negative memes and therefore can fully express my individual viewpoint and create what I choose, when I choose to do it. The other figures represent society which is bound by countless negative memes. Not only are they bound by their individual negative memes, they are bound together by their shared negative meme chords. In order to live instead of trying to survive, cut the memes that bind you, and live life to the fullest!

avoiding people with dogs, parks, and beaches where dogs are allowed. This meme would remain with you until you delved deep inside your own psyche and cleaned out those old agreements that no longer serve you.

When you say that someone is a free spirit, what that really means is that they are literally free. They are not bound by as many memes as the majority of the people on this planet. A meme is an idea, symbol, or practice transmitted from one mind to another through speech, gestures, rituals, or any other method of communication. It's an agreement that you believe to be true or real regardless of whether it is in fact real or not.

Think of a meme as something imitated, copied, or passed down through generations, usually without conscious thought. Some people describe memes as the cultural analog of genes. Memes interestingly enough replicate, mutate, spread, and often behave just like a virus you can't avoid. Think of organized religion, politics, fashion, and music. Memes are ideas spread from generation to generation and from person to person, that we often take as unquestioned truth. We believe them, and after all everyone else knows and believes the same thing. Some memes spread and thrive over time, while others slowly become extinct. What Darwin wrote about survival of the fittest applies to memes.

Let's look at some interesting memes.

- *Meat is bad for you.*
- *Pork is the other white meat.*
- *Prejudice is wrong with respect to race or gender, but acceptable in terms of stupidity or social status.*
- *Some sexual acts are moral, some are immoral, and some are disgusting; which ones belong to which category changes over time.*
- *An individual's vote makes a difference.*

- *God exists, is omniscient, omnipotent, omnibeneficient, at least to believers.*
- *The Bible, Torah or Koran is the inspired word of God – literal and infallible.*
- *Marriage, birth, and death must be sanctified by the church, temple, mosque or synagogue.*
- *If you pray in just the right way, you'll go to Heaven or other good things will happen.*
- *The terrorists responsible for the 9/11 tragedy believed that Americans are evil, and if the terrorists kill them and die in the process, they will become martyrs, go to heaven and perhaps will get 72 virgins.*

Are they true? Not necessarily, yet through whatever mechanism, we start to believe they are and start to act based on those beliefs. Become aware of the memes by which you live your life: the ideas, symbols, and concepts that give you a mind-jerk reaction to something that's like a knee-jerk reaction on a spiritual level.

Are you aware of your memes and how they've changed your behavior? Are these the memes you want? When you become aware, you improve your ability to sculpt your own thoughts and your own life. The first step in awareness is to look at how you look at things. The second is to understand the fundamental memes that have been transmitted and instilled in you by society, culture, and family. It doesn't really matter how you acquired the meme. What matters is that you recognize what a meme is and which ones you choose to keep and discard.

Can you list the things you believe?

_____

_____

_____

_____

_____

_____

_____

_____

_____

Are they true? How do you know they are true? What if the opposite was true? How would your life change then? We often hear the term comfort zone. Memes tend to keep you in your comfort zone whether they serve you well or cause negativity and even illness. In order to change your life, you must be willing to get out of your comfort zone.

While I am somewhat influenced by societal meme chords, I know what they are and how to work around them. I choose consciously which memes I want to hold onto, and which memes to discard. I always retain my ability to freely choose which decision I will make here and now. In order for G.O.D particles to join forces and work together for the greatest good of all, they need shared meme chord. There are certain memes that are in place for logical and organizational purposes. For example, drive when the light is green and stop when it's red. This helps to have a somewhat logical and workable way to travel. This does not mean that they're set in stone. There are shared meme chords of humanity today.

Unfortunately, the majority of our society is so bound by memes, one after the other and before you know it, each person begins to look like he is so tightly wound with rope in so many directions that he can barely move. That is how so many people merely exist in life instead of truly living life to the fullest.

We now have a society that lives in fear instead of love. We have created a fear-based reality and continue to impose this reality on ourselves and on our children. If someone does not believe or does not subscribe to this mentality and reality, they are ridiculed, made fun of, and sometimes punished for it. Oftentimes, we are punishing those people who understand freedom at their very core and choose to live their lives accordingly.

I am free because I choose to be free. This means that I consciously removed most of the memes imposed by my parents, school and society in general. I also do not subscribe to any religious dogmas, limitations of any kind, or expectations and programming from anyone but myself. I am also free to think, to question, and to create whatever I choose whenever I choose to do it. I am free to imagine, to feel, and to express myself. If I don't feel like doing something, I just don't do it. It's really that simple. You can have this kind of freedom too.

Let's look at some memes that affect entire species of animals. If an antelope in the bush of Africa sees another antelope being eaten by a lion, it will form an agreement that lions eat antelopes. Bingo, program in place. Now the other antelopes will subscribe to that meme and since energy is always interconnected and information is shared instantly, all the other antelopes all over the world will subscribe to that same meme. Other lions will also form the agreement or meme that they should eat antelopes and again, the other lions from all over the world will subscribe to that same meme. Some memes become a part of the species and are passed down to other generations through cellular memory. Karma naturally follows, etc.

For example, if I don't feel like doing something or going somewhere, I won't. My husband has a meme that dictates that he must be socially polite and attend all "important" functions. I don't have this meme by choice. It was a very difficult concept for him to understand about me. When I was a little girl in school, and memes were being implanted into my fellow students, I couldn't understand why the other kids did not question anything. They accepted without questioning or hesitation and committed to memory as they were told every single meme. I had a million questions and was promptly told to sit down, be quiet, and do what everyone else was doing. As you can imagine it never worked out for them because even as a child, I was still me.

I did not accept many memes from my parents. I do however choose to keep some I got from my dad. Some of them are: Guns are good for self-defense. I can do anything I set my mind to. Anything a man can do, I can do better and faster. I must always be self-sufficient and never depend on any man for anything. My mind is free and irrepressible, and that is my divine right and is a part of our original blueprint. The mind can be opened, closed, programmed and reprogrammed. There are many different tools available in that department. I personally prefer to do my own programming and reprogramming instead of allowing society, television, religions, parents or government do it for me.

Today, unfortunately the human race is kept in a constant state of fear by our government, by our religious leaders, whether at work or at home. Fear is the easiest way to control the masses and keep them in a limited vision, kind of like horses with blinders on. It is time to remove those blinders and see everyone and everything as they truly are. There are meme chords in place throughout the hierarchy of creation, from our galaxy to the microcosms. Some of these memes are vital to our existence and evolution, while others are toxic and only serve to harm. Ultimately, it's up to you which memes you wish to keep and which ones you want to discard.

Overview

Freedom is frequency and it is always your choice. You decide which memes you do and do not subscribe to. If a meme no longer serves you, then cut it and let it go. There are many positive memes that you can create and subscribe to. Positive memes vibrate on a high frequency. For example, you can agree to always be healthy and wealthy. That is a good meme. Whatever you touch turns to gold, is another good meme. You are the creator of your own universe is a meme that everyone should subscribe to. Bottom line is, you must use your discretion in auditing your memes. Although there are certain meme chords that we all subscribe to in order to have order in our universe, the personal ones are those that we should inspect and evaluate and then reevaluate every so often. Memes are programs so if you want to reprogram any part of your life, examine the memes or programs that you have put in place in that particular part of your life.

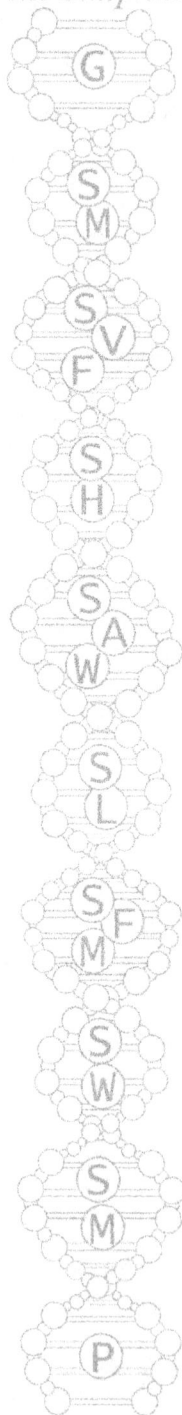

Chapter 8
Words of Success
The Blueprint

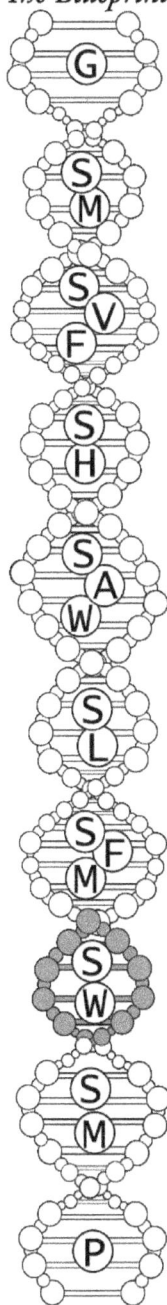

The Blueprint

Abracadabra. This word is a phrase, which comes from the ancient Aramaic incantation Avra Kehdabra, meaning "I will create as I speak" or "I will create with my words." This incantation was used as a magic formula to heal the sick and protect against illness and misfortune. Some even posted these words on their doorways for the same purpose. Words have tremendous power and energy and must be considered carefully before spoken or written. Words are encoded energetically so your words are codes you use to program your life. You bring things into your physical life by speaking them because the energy of words is broadcast out into the cosmos. Words spoken out loud are even more powerful than your thoughts alone. The written word carries the seal of permanence.

I Shall Create as I Speak

Speech is an interesting concept. Before language was invented, human beings were able to look at one another and the universe around them and instantly feel that energy. They knew in an instant if they were looking at a friend or foe. They sensed which animal was dangerous and which leaf was poisonous. They were one with all of creation. Back then human beings had to be their true authentic selves because there was no mechanism to hide it. Then speech was invented and that brought on a whole new era of deceit, trickery, valances, and other human games wherein we hide who we really are or better yet, pretend to be something that we are not. Oh the games we play through the sounds coming out of our mouths.

Your words are alive and they are powerful! They have energy and volition. The power of the spoken or written word is so much more than people currently think. Words can kill and words can heal. This is absolutely accurate and must be carefully considered before we utter a single syllable. We have already established that your thoughts are things, and that they are alive and have volition. When your thoughts form words and expressed through sound, it actually travels directly to the person you are speaking to and energetically affects him. What you say is equivalent to placing an order with a cosmic menu. Make no mistake about it. You will get exactly what you order every single time. Depending on how you say what you say and depending on your vibrational frequency, you may actually be making a decree without even realizing it.

For thousands of years people were taught to pray. Then churches came about and you were taught to pray in groups. Although I am not a fan of organized religion, they did get something right. Prayer, especially group prayer really works because it is your thoughts transmuted into words that are broadcast out into the universe along with everyone else's that is with you in that group.

There is strength in numbers, not only physically, but spiritually as well. When you combine and unite your words and energy with the words and energy of others, the resulting energy becomes very powerful and manifests rather quickly in physical reality.

Mainstream religions use words to pray. Wiccans use words for spells. Monarchs and political leaders use words to make decrees and to brainwash their subjects or voters. When these words are delivered from the perspective of authority and with an air of truthfulness, whether these words are actually true or not is irrelevant. They will come across as truth and they will manifest in physical reality. Words are the finest mechanism known to man for the purpose of programming and reprogramming the human mind. Words are a powerful healing tool and an extremely dangerous weapon. How you use your words is of course your choice.

Words of "Modern" Society

Words are a medium used to create memes. It is not the only medium but it is a powerful one. Verbal memes are based on the culture and society, and the meaning and associated word memes change with the times. For example, today you hear teenagers saying, "That's sick!" for something that is great. This is confusing to the universe and the meme becomes convoluted. So, when you say this phrase, it may bring about a Great Sickness.

Memes or agreements change over time but if the same word is used for more than one meaning, we must really consider carefully which words we choose to say for the end result we are trying to bring about.

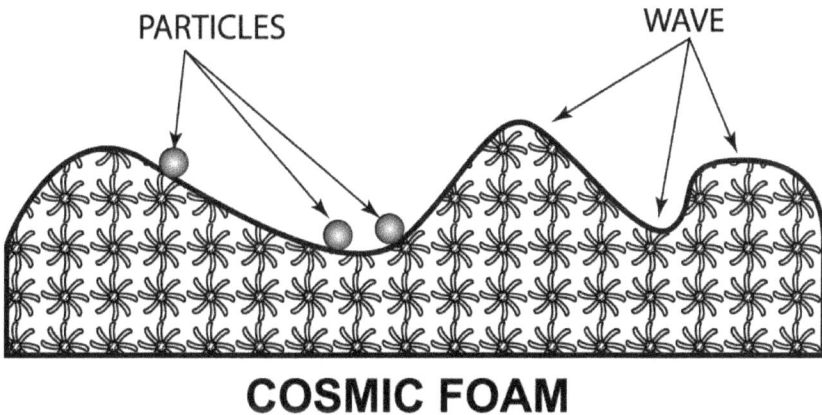

PARTICLES   WAVE

COSMIC FOAM

When you place attention on something, cosmic waveforms and cosmic foam transmute into particles, which manifests what you are paying attention to as matter in your physical reality. Words create matter.

Many people are not aware of the power of the word and are therefore not conscious of what they say or the consequences and actions following their words. People will say, "I am as serious as a heart attack" or "Something is so beautiful, you could die" and "I am sick and tired of ..." and other such phrases. A common popular phrase today is, "You're the bomb" for someone who is great, beautiful, hot, etc. Depending on whom you are saying it to and their frequency and resulting state of health, they may literally blow up or something in their bodies can blow up. So a phrase like "You're the bomb" can quite literally cause a heart attack. Some people also say "I need more money." "I need a vacation." Well, guess what? If that's what you say, the universe will send you more "need." You ordered and it will be sent.

Lies or Untruths

The universe does not discriminate. What you think and say is what you get. If you say something, it is interpreted as the truth. There is no such thing as an untruth because there is no objective reality. If you make up a lie to get you out of something or into something, think before you lie because it will happen. You have the power of thought and the power of the word. In fact when you write something down, you make it permanent. It's a permanent decree. You make decrees all the time without even realizing it. It's one of the universal truths and part of The Blueprint.

Decrees

When you initiate the power of decree, G.O.D particles join forces to bring you what you want. It is like the might of the universe is aligned behind it. Affirmations and prayers are typically repeated by the way. A decree is like making a demand of the universe. Decrees are made only once. You make unconscious decrees all the time without even realizing it. I suggest doing it consciously. Here is an example of a conscious intentional decree.

- *Example 1.* By Divine Decree, in the name of G.O.D, under grace, I invoke the power of the cosmos to now transmute every negative thought, belief, pattern, condition, attachment or alliance that I have made, and so it is.

- *Example 2.* In the name of all that is light, under grace, I decree that all memes that no longer serve me, that have held me down, kept me in bondage and in limited vision, are now cut and eliminated, from this lifetime and every other lifetime. So be it.

- *Example 3.* By the power of all creation, under grace, I now call forth all my angels to bring me the energy of pure unconditional love of higher consciousness to earth. It is done.

Human beings are only too eager to give away their power to anyone and everyone. Whoever talks to them has the potential to get their power including gang leaders, cult leaders, religious leaders, government, police, criminals, strangers, gurus, you name it. Children are taught to give away their power early on in life. Freedom became a nice idea in our world but is nothing more than an illusion. There are approximately 8 billion people on this planet. There is strength in numbers. If every human being decided to join forces with the rest of the human race and used the power of thought and the power of words, then perhaps we could create a better world.

You have the power of creation and manifestation within you. Remember there are trillions of G.O.D particles that make up the galaxy that is you. They are all ready, willing, and able to create whatever you order. Be careful in using your power because if you use it unethically over others, you will generate the same karma for yourself. We all have free will and we must be careful not to infringe on the free will of our fellow human beings. This would be considered force, which is a negative use of power. Power is positively charged, whereas force is negatively charged. Each will generate appropriate karma and consequences.

Your inner power or lack of it is projected out from within the galaxy that is you, and all of creation will know and feel whether you're coming from a place of power and strength, or weakness and negative force for that matter. They will respond to you accordingly and mirror that back to you. Basically, if people think they can take advantage of you, they will. It is your doing and your creation. If that happened to you in the past, look at the situation you created, why you created it, what you learned, and let it go. It is what it is. Then move on.

Overview

When you speak, it's like placing an order from a cosmic menu. The energy of your words will bring what you're saying to your physical life. Your words have the power to heal and the power to kill. Choose your words wisely and carefully. This applies to human communication as well. The words that come out of your mouth are difficult to take back and like a ripple effect, will affect not only the person you're speaking to, but everyone around him, and everyone around the next person and so forth.

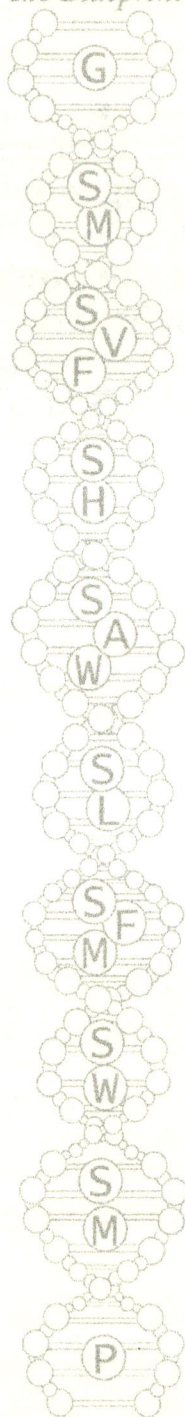

The Blueprint

114

Chapter 9
Success in Sex and Marriage

The Blueprint

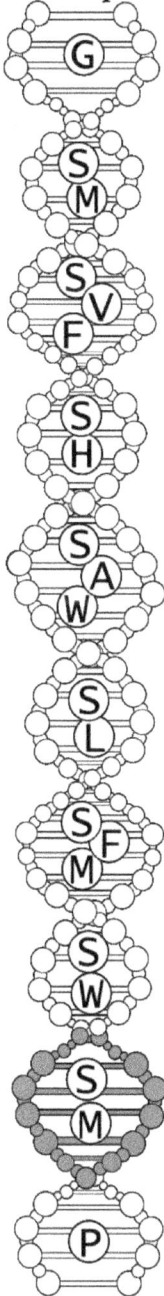

The Blueprint

Sex and marriage typically go hand in hand. However, both sex and marriage have been misunderstood and misconstrued for thousands of years. Sex is natural, beautiful, and vital to life, health, and happiness for all adult human beings. Marriage is an integral part of The Blueprint because absolutely every single male and female energy in creation seeks marriage. It is G.O.D energy and since the cosmic orgasm when it separated, it constantly seeks to reunite. It is all a part of the Great Omnipotent Design! Everything in creation is also cyclical.

Like a cosmic orgasm when the energy expands and contracts, so does every marriage. At times it expands and couples grow apart, and it contracts when couples get closer together. It is natural and fantastic. During the times of the expansion, use this time to grow as an individual and during the times of contraction, use this time to grow closer together and strengthen your bond. There is feminine energy in all men, and male energy in all women. So regardless of your preference of a sexual partner sex is much more than just two physical organic bodies coming together. The physical act of sex is only the beginning. A loving sexual union is a merging of the souls and electromagnetic fields. Marriage requires love, commitment, and mutual respect and it must be maintained by your attention. What we don't pay attention to ceases to exist.

Sexual Relationships

An intimate sexual relationship between two people can and should be magical especially if those people love each other. Unfortunately it is not always the case. Today so many people have trust issues that it is extremely difficult for them to be intimate. Instead they use sex as a diversion for getting close. In a typical sexual close encounter, you begin to feel aroused and excited with sexual energy, then instead of exploring each other intimately and spiritually, you kill your spiritual switch, put on your body armor and have primitive, shallow genital sex. Now don't get me wrong, because sex for the sake of sex is fine. In fact it is one of my favorite exercises and pastimes. However once you have experienced a cosmic orgasm it becomes very difficult to settle for anything else.

The kind of sexual experience I am talking about can only be described as the art of ecstasy. It rejuvenates and regenerates every cell in your body and gives you incomparable energy. This magical sex gives you wings and allows you to soar long after the physical sexual act is over. It literally makes you high, because the frequency you are in at that time is extremely high. It is an intentional connection on all levels, a deep, full physical and spiritual connection in which all the G.O.D particles of the soul, body, and mind come together to create ecstasy. Your vibrational frequency is in harmony with that of your partner, and as you come together you create an electromagnetic high vibrating energy that is beyond words. Like a propulsion mechanism, it makes you feel like you are spinning out into outer space a million miles per minute. This kind of sexual experience can be compared to savoring rare fine wine, whereas, the shallow, genital sex is like drinking plain, cheap, boring beer.

So why do the majority of people go through life without ever experiencing this state of ecstasy? There is a logical explanation as to why they don't, and it can be changed. What happens is your fear and your memes get in the way. These memes create barriers or walls around you and you may be unable to connect on such a deep level. The second reason would be because you and your partner are not vibrating on the same frequency. Another important factor to consider is that your sexual history affects your entire being and any issues that you may have are broadcast loud and clear throughout your body and the cosmos. It is therefore important to clean it up at your earliest convenience. Sexuality like everything else is a frequency, a current. Cleaning up your past is simple. Everything that happens in life is your doing. Go back in time, review your experiences, and see why you created them and what you learned from each one. Forgive yourself and move on. That is history. You are in the here and now.

Roots of Sexual Repression

Initially churches (all religious institutions and places of worship) were created as clubs and business organizations. Their purpose was to control the masses through religion and to suppress spiritual development. This was also a great way to create a hierarchy and establish the pecking order. In order for the patriarchal society to come into full power they had to find a way to shift consciousness and suppress the feminine power and energy. So they chose female sexuality and began a brilliant marketing campaign. Hence, a sexual meme was born. Prior to that, women knew their power, intuition, and conscious connection to all life, and while they had desire to create life, they understood that they never had to conceive a child if it was not their intention.

Churches cleverly began promoting sex for procreation only. Women were forced to believe the only reason they had to have sex was to produce babies, and that they had no control over the birthing process. Aside from procreation, sex was promoted as something bad, dirty, and disgusting. Women were further brainwashed into believing that sex was something they had to put up with to serve men. Women began to believe this propaganda and many still do. That is also how women came to believe that sex can only be performed within the rights of marriage. This is another meme, which still affects society today.

Wow, what a brilliant marketing strategy, and it is obviously very effective. Once programming was in place all they had to do to keep it in place was maintenance. New marketing campaigns with new and improved promotional fear tactics were introduced to create an even greater fear of sexuality and self-expression. Say hello to sexually transmitted diseases (STDs) and related illnesses: AIDS, herpes, syphilis, gonorrhea, and HPV (Human Papilloma Virus), which could result in various cancers and other illnesses. There are many more but I'm sure you are getting my point. New STDs are added constantly lest we forget the fear factor. You can read about these diseases in newspapers, see commercials on TV, on the radio, and online. Of course it would scare you out of your mind and you become horrified at the mere thought of sexual expression and intimacy. The earth's collective consciousness frequency is at an all time low as a result of this sexual repression meme.

Since I am on this subject, I would like to address religions that require their followers to cover their heads and even faces. Both men and women are required to wear various head coverings all the time. In some religions, when women get married they cut their hair or shave their heads and wear wigs. Then there is my personal favorite, the burka. Let's just cover the whole face, why don't we? Unbelievable! This is all done they say for modesty, humility, and as a reminder that God is watching. This pure nonsense is really enforced so that they can keep you disconnected from G.O.D because you are both a transmitter and receiver of energy, and the crown chakra on top of your head is your connection to spirituality and higher consciousness. It is your connection to the source and to the truth. Let's not forget religious practices where people have to wear magic underwear, or have sex only after you are married through a sheet with a hole in it. OK, that is kind of funny but in a really sad sort of way.

When churches programmed humanity with the implant that sex is bad, human beings became sealed off from their cosmic connection. This disconnection keeps human beings suppressed, mostly blind, and therefore much easier to control and manipulate. Once again, these are just some of the ridiculous tactics religions use to promote suppression of humanity.

The Art of Sexual Expression

Through sexuality with intent to connect spiritually, human beings can remember who they are and reconnect with G.O.D because the ecstatic frequency of cosmic orgasm connects you with all information. The physical body is designed for sexual pleasure and that creates frequencies that heal and rejuvenate the body. Sexuality looks at itself as a creator and invokes a spiritual freedom, which like a bridge can transport you to higher consciousness. This however can only be achieved with a partner in a monogamous fully bonded relationship. When you have multiple partners you do not fully connect and bond with any one of them, and men scatter their energy and seed, while women take in various seed and frequencies. This typically causes chaos in her physical body as well as her spiritual universe. It is best to be in one relationship at a time and when that relationship is over, then move on to the next one.

The more intense orgasms you experience, the higher your electrical current gets and the greater intensity of orgasm you can experience because the central nervous system is able to handle higher ecstatic frequencies. When you are ready you will begin to experience cosmic orgasms. The central nervous system determines how you express yourself and how you feel, and if it is not very evolved, your sexual experience will be very limited because the nervous system conducts the electrical current. The orgasm is vital to your health because it heals and realigns the physical body. You are electromagnetic beings and when you physically merge with another human being, you bond your electromagnetic frequencies together. When your frequencies are in sync and vibrating on a love frequency, true magic happens!

Bodily fluids are extremely potent energetically and when they connect, interchange or are ingested, they imprint you physically and spiritually. When you take in or come into contact with bodily fluids, you are actually harnessing that energy which creates a very strong bond between the couple. During the sexual union both people

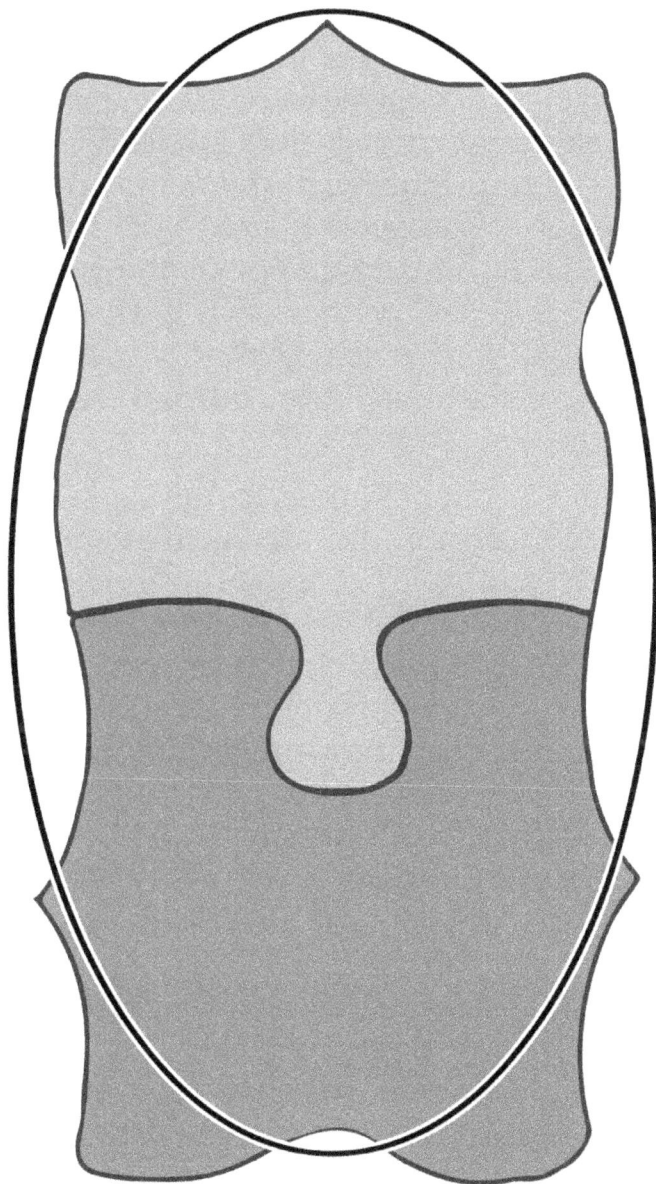

The monogamous sexual union or marriage which over time forms a strong, trusting bond which can become a sexual link and can result in the ultimate cosmic orgasm. This is the stuff that fairy tales are made of and can be compared to savoring fabulous fine wine.

pick up each other's frequency, including thoughts, feelings, and mood. Once in a while you may be fortunate enough to have sex with someone who is energetically powerful, spiritually clean and clear and vibrates on a super high frequency. When you enter their electromagnetic field you will feel a high that is incomparable to anything else out there. You will feel your own energy rising to match that of your partner. That is the ultimate natural high that lasts for days if not weeks afterwards.

Sexual intimacy should be fun and fabulous. Explore each other intimately with every part of the body. Most people will explore very little and it will be limited to oral sex, followed by shallow genital sex. I am suggesting that you use every inch of your body for exploration. The entire physical body is one big erogenous zone from the top of the head to the toes on your feet. Ultimately though, sexual ecstasy begins and ends in the mind. Kiss and touch everything and everywhere. As long as both partners are comfortable with each other, then nothing is off limits. I can't even imagine telling my husband that he can only touch this part or that part of my body. He would probably think I'm crazy. My entire body is completely available to him at all times. The same goes for me. I can explore, touch, feel, and lick anything anywhere on his body. This makes sex a fun adventure every time. You can become aroused from one word or one touch in the least likely of places. You can use one finger and one touch to transfer an electrical volt that would put Viagra out of business.

Take a few minutes and think about what memes you have in place that bind and prohibit you from experiencing the ultimate sexual ecstasy. Write them down. No one will see them. It's just for you.

_____

_____

_____

_____

_____

_____

_____

_____

_____

Come back to this section and look at it in 30 days. See if any of these memes are gone. My hunch is after you finish reading this book and begin to reconnect with all that is, your sex life will be on an entirely new level.

The art of self-pleasure is very important. You can learn to use the energy that would stimulate you sexually without giving it away to another person. You are G.O.D comprised of trillions of G.O.D particles. You owe it to all of them to feel pleasure. You should not have to wait for someone else to give you pleasure when you can do it yourself. There is a time and place for all kinds of sexual pleasure. Sometimes it's great to pleasure yourself and sometimes it's great to do it with a partner. Sometimes it's great to pleasure yourself while your partner watches. Your partner will find this quite arousing you I assure you. There are no rules and no right and wrong. It is all about getting pleasure and being happy.

Marriage

Marriage can be a fairytale or a nightmare, but either way it is much more than the union of two people. Marriage is a universal bonding relationship that unites the male and female energies into a whole. According to the cosmic blueprint all male and female energies seek this marriage. If you look at the marriage of everything in creation from atoms to planets, you will find that each possesses a consciousness and is either positively or negatively charged, meaning it is either male or female and always seeks marriage. All G.O.D particles, which are the building blocks of everything are either male or female and never deviate from the one-to-one ratio and always seek marriage. An interesting part of The Blueprint is that all male and female energies in the universe are seeking stability or neutrality. Meaning, they seek to return to the energy of purpose. Thus, marriage is a universal principle used to unite all male and female energies. This is true regardless if it is a heterosexual relationship or homosexual relationship, because there is feminine energy in all males and male energy in all females.

I would like to clarify some misconceptions about marriage. Marriage is not about ownership.

Some couples get married and then feel like they have ownership rights over their spouse. This is a weak and toxic approach to marriage, which can only come from personal insecurity. Marriage is not about what can I get out of him or her. It is also not about what have you done for me lately? Marriage is definitely not about waiting for your spouse to make you happy. If that's the case, good luck. You will be waiting for a lifetime and then you will leave this planet very disappointed.

Marriage is a union of two individuals who over time create a strong loving bond. It is a merger of two energies that over time become one. Marriage is about love, honor, and respect and what that means is giving your spouse understanding, room to grow as an individual, support and inspiration. It is a true partnership in which you and your spouse fit together like two puzzle pieces. Marriage like everything else is cyclical, so learn to enjoy growing closer, then moving apart, and then growing closer again. We are all a product of a cosmic orgasm and we and everything in our lives mirror the pattern of that cosmic orgasm.

The sexual part of your marriage is extremely important. Those people who vibrate on a very high frequency cannot get close or be with someone who is not operating on the same frequency or voltage. They simply don't fit and they don't merge energetically. It's like oil and water. It's not comfortable. When a couple has been together for some time, they begin to vibrate on the same or on similar frequencies. This means that they give each other vibrational nourishment and sexual linking. To sexually link means to merge with someone who is moving at the same or a compatible voltage rate. Over time you become vibrationally hooked to your spouse and that depth of two people coming together and linking in this capacity is what everyone craves.

Infidelity

Infidelity has become very commonplace in today's culture. Each relationship is different with its own dynamics and it is always a personal choice. This is simply something to consider. When one individual in a marriage chooses to sexually engage with another person, it disturbs the energetic balance and harmony of the marriage. It also changes the vibrational frequency of each individual. Imagine plugging in to a receptacle and it's defective. It will blow your fuse and short the circuit. It also creates another thing, another physical relationship, and you start to place a part of your focus and attention on this new relationship, thereby giving less attention to the current one.

What you don't pay attention to and maintain ceases to exist. It disappears. You then bring your new frequency into your bed with your spouse. You are no longer compatible with the frequency of your spouse and you will be repulsed by one another energetically. It will eventually stabilize but if you continue to do this, you will be

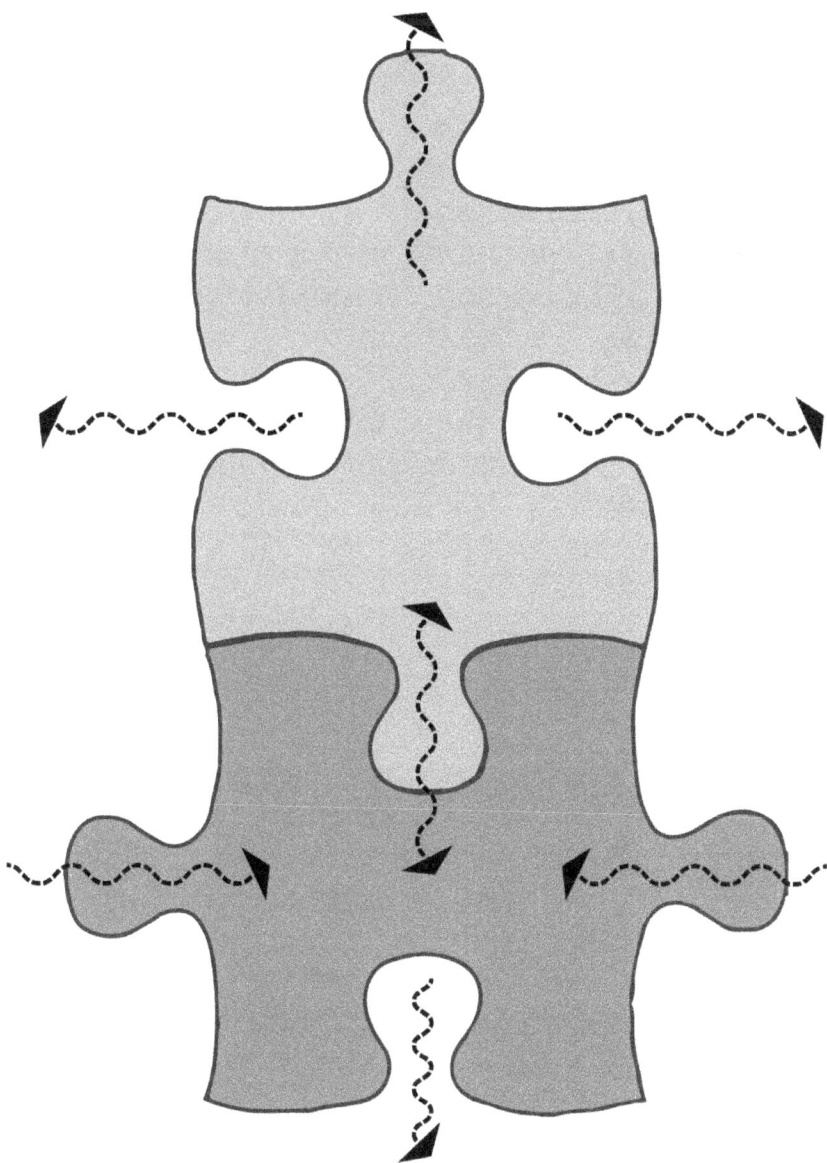

The non-committed union or marriage, wherein your seed is scattered, your energy is spread and convoluted. Neither of the unions is getting enough attention to make it a real and satisfying, deep spiritual and physical connection and orgasm. This is the primitive, shallow genital sex like drinking plain, warm beer.

miserable because neither relationship will have stability and will not fully exist in the physical. You are also disturbing the natural order of things. According to the cosmic blueprint, everything in creation is meant to be a one-to-one relationship. The solution is simple. Be in one relationship at a time. Give your current relationship or marriage your undivided attention and enjoy the ride. If and when it is over, move on. Then you are free to create new relationships and bond with other individuals. If you follow this formula, you will be operating from a place of power rather than desperation and neediness.

Overview

Sex and marriage are the very foundation our civilization is built on. If they are both approached with love, honor, and dignity our entire culture will improve drastically. People who are happily married tend to be healthier, wealthier and more stable. A happy marriage with a deeply fulfilling sex life creates magic in every area of your life. This is very important because when you have a true partner in life, you feel secure knowing that no matter what happens, you have someone who will always be there for you. You know that someone has your back so to speak. Plus, universal laws dictate that you cannot fail if at least one other person believes in you.

Marriage without sex is unhealthy. If an adult individual does not have a healthy and frequent sex life, over time, he will have very little lifeforce available to him. It is unnatural for human beings who are adults to live without sex. The choice of celibacy for religious reasons is silly and unreasonable. Clearly, it does not work. I am certain we all know how hard the Vatican tries to hide and sweep under the rug, the sexual abuse of boys and men that has been going on since the creation of the church, and continues inside those walls today.

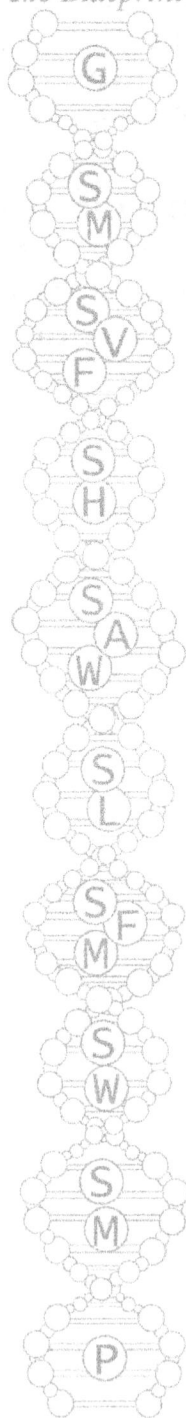

Chapter 10
Success in Parenting-Raising Healthy Successful Children

The Blueprint

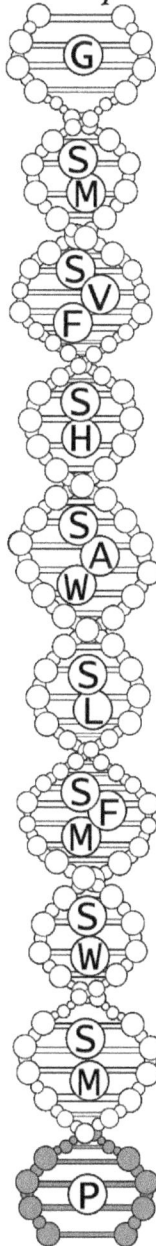

The Blueprint

Parenting is the most important responsibility we have. Everything we say and everything we do or don't do serves as a lesson to our children one way or another. Children do not come with instruction manuals so many of us simply try to do the best with what we have, based on our own viewpoint, upbringing, and memes. Raising healthy, happy, and responsible children is not something that happens by accident. It requires love, patience, and attention on our parts. Aside from our own evolution, there is nothing more important than treating this responsibility with the highest regard.

Children are little miracles. They are baby G.O.Ds and we must learn to treat them with the same kind of respect, honor, and integrity that we want for ourselves. We teach by example. Our children may currently be occupying smaller bodies than us, but that in no way means that they are any less intelligent or powerful than we are. The most valuable gift you can give your children outside of your love is freedom. Freedom from your beliefs, fears, and memes, and freedom to make their own choices and to express themselves in their authentic natural way. We as parents are here to love them, to guide them, and to teach them to make good choices. Children

are already born with wings. We must help them to spread their wings, then step back and let them fly!

Our Children are Little G.O.Ds

Children should be given every chance and opportunity for freedom in every way so that they can create their own lives and realities of their choosing. It is important for children to be raised with loving, gentle guidance and predictable discipline. They should be informed of consequences for their actions, then we, as parents must follow through if and when the opportunity presents itself. I think children need a predictable discipline system during the early development years. I also suggest that you encourage them to explore their natural gifts and abilities. My children dislike restriction, dictatorship, and loss of personal freedom. I raised them to be this way. Therefore, they make choices based on their desired outcome.

I don't necessarily believe in punishment. I simply correct their behavior, enforce the consequences that are in place and move on. I don't believe in dwelling on negative behaviors for too long because what you feed grows. Instead I choose to acknowledge the positive and use a reward system to validate what I want more of. You should teach your children to be confident and have the highest regard for themselves. I respect my children for their wisdom as much as they

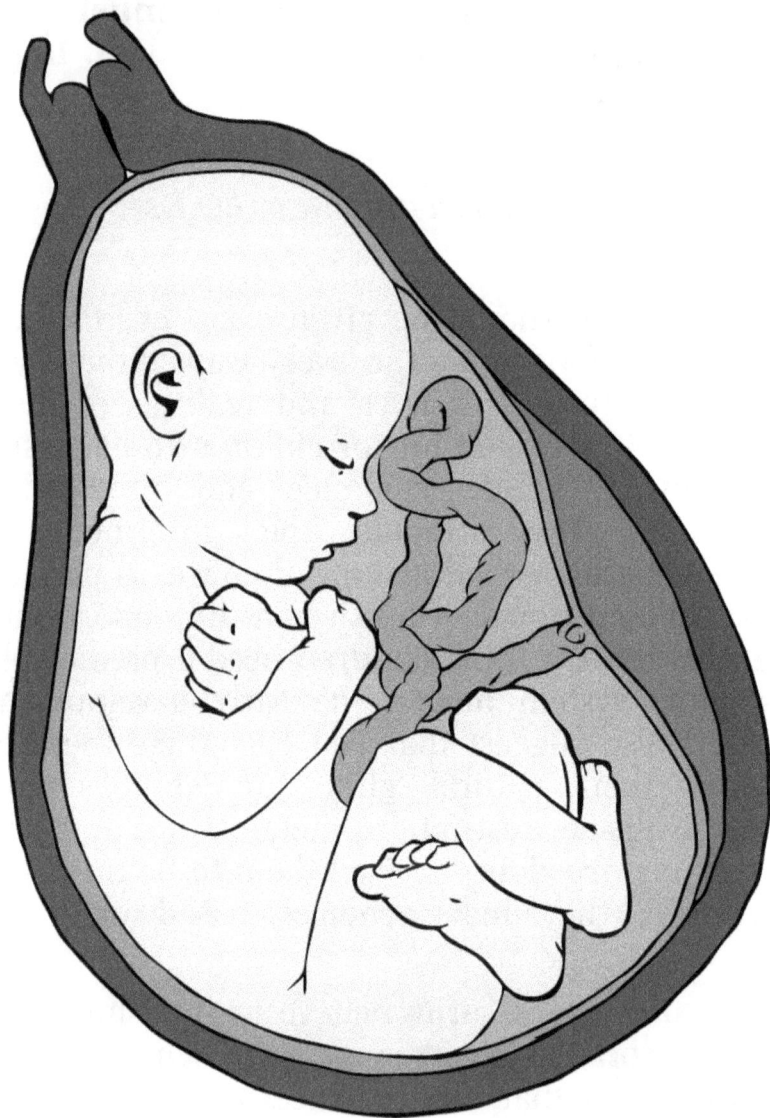

Your child comes in from a sleep-like state and as you can see from his torus or donut shape position, he is closed spiritually and physically. The mother must lovingly teach her child to open up and spread his wings, and ensure that he doesn't end up being bound by negative memes, which society and religion will try to impose upon him.

136

respect me for mine. When we have disagreements, we talk about them and share our viewpoints with one another. I learn from them as much as they learn from me.

Get to Know Your Child Early

It is important to try and understand who is being born as your child and what the purpose is of the coming life. A mother, for instance, should make a point of trying to find out what name the incoming person wants to call themselves, since a person's name is an expression of not only their spiritual development, but has meaning relating to the path of education and purpose that they are on. Think of the incoming being as a person who has lived other lifetimes and is beginning a new one for a specific reason. They had many lives before and are now coming out of a sleep-like state to start another life. Age is completely irrelevant because the being coming in to be your child may have had more lives and physical experiences than you. If you think that you are better, smarter, or somehow more advanced than someone younger than you, then you are completely wrong.

When a woman becomes pregnant, she opens a window of opportunity so that a being may come back into the physical world. The decision as to which woman the being will come into is not entirely up to the being, although there is a tendency for us to stay within the same family. It is therefore possible that your grandfather may become your granddaughter. The mechanism of parent selection depends on the life purpose of the being coming into the body, as does karma.

Once a woman becomes pregnant, within three weeks the incoming being will decide whether or not to inhabit the new body that is being created. The mother and father both contribute some of their genes in forming the physical body for the incoming person. Later as the brain is forming, the incoming being will send impulses to signify how many brain connectors to create. This process is very important because the brain, once it is formed, must be able to handle the wisdom the being is carrying from the many accumulated lifetimes. Once the brain is developed, the being then transfers a copy of all of its wisdom into the acids of the brain where it will reside.

During the following months of pregnancy, if the mother vibrates on a high frequency, she will receive signals or information regarding the path of learning that the being she is carrying is on. Your child may be coming in clean and clear or plagued with hostilities and anger from unresolved issues from a previous physical life. During the pregnancy, the mother should try to contemplate and feel as much about the child coming in as possible so that she can have a clearer understanding of how to assist them in their new life.

Your Child is Not Your Personal Property

As difficult as this may sound, you should try not to feel possessive about your child because he is not your personal property. You should also not guide your children to an image you hold of them. Instead teach them that life is about self-expression and they are free to make their own choices, but with your guidance. If we stop for an instant and view our children as people on a path of discovery and learning of their own, we might start to find some explanations for behavior that we are not able to understand and personality traits that don't make sense to us. If we recognize that these are people who lived lives before, and have brought forward wisdom from previous lives, we can begin to understand why we all have different aptitudes and different levels of intelligence and knowledge.

We are all on our own paths of discovery and learning, and need different information at different times in order to continue growing. We do not learn the same lessons in life at the same time, so we must learn to give each other space to seek out answers to questions that are needed for our continued spiritual growth. Think of our world as the school of life. Some of us are learning kindergarten level life lessons. Whereas, others are taking graduate school level life courses.

Once your child is born, it is important that you help them to understand who they are and why they are here. The first ten years of your child's life are extremely important for their emotional development and they should get as much love and guidance from you as possible. You should also be helping your child at this time, to gain complete understanding of who they are and the path of growth that they are on. In other words, they need to understand the meaning and purpose of their life, before they embark on their own life journey. Only positive influences and environments should be provided during these years, so they can become completely secure, self-confident and well balanced.

Today most people do not have an understanding of how to handle their children correctly from a spiritual perspective. Instead we are simply born and thrown into a hostile world and forced to create defensive emotions and behavior patterns in order to survive. Our children live in a world controlled by toxic men, who happen to be the meme enforcers of modern day. These men of power seek control over others because they operate on the low frequency of greed. It is imperative that we properly educate and prepare our children early on in life, how to live within this system, but how not to become a victim of it.

Development and Education

The next 10 years of your child's life should be spent on spiritual growth and development, while learning to use their imagination and willpower. As young adults, your children should be taught to find a balance between work and time for creativity and spiritual growth. For example, my children were taught early on in life to spend 50% of their time on schoolwork, chores and other responsibilities. The remaining time is spent on various creative activities, including but not limited to socializing, art, reading, music and simply being in nature and reflecting on the living library of earth.

I teach my children to take 100% responsibility for themselves and their choices, rather than relying on a mythical god, idol or any other outside entity. They are taught to communicate with their higher consciousness that guides each being in the cosmos. Only through understanding and cognition of The Blueprint, can our children evolve to higher forms of consciousness.

We as parents must teach our children how to manage their lives and how to earn things. It is important to teach our children lessons on a gradient, which are age appropriate. For example, when I wanted to teach my children about drug abuse, at 8 years of age, I taught them that drugs were bad regardless of what form they came in. When my children turned 13, I brought home books and videos, which described in great detail the effects of drug abuse. By the time my son turned 17, I took him to a drug rehabilitation center so that he could see first hand what drug abuse does to a person and their family. I also took him to the cemetery so that he could see where drug abuse can lead to.

Since they were little my children had reward boards with little star stickers and for every positive action they got a star. They also got stars for good grades, reading books, being responsible, respectful and generous. My children know that their real inheritance is the transfer of values and wisdom that they are getting from their parents.

Practical Skills

Learning practical skills at an early age will give your children a competitive edge. It is important to teach them the rules of the game in our physical world. This includes personal hygiene, money management, social awareness and self-defense. Engage your children when you are cooking in the kitchen so that they can learn to cook for themselves. Invite them to dinner with you and teach them social skills. Ask them to join you when you are paying your monthly bills and teach them about money management.

Overview

Treat your children with respect. Speak to them the same way you would speak to an intelligent adult. Most importantly, listen to your children. They know and feel when you're really listening

and when you care about what they have to say. Guide and nourish them, but allow them to have room to make their own choices. Make sure your children know that they can talk to you about anything and everything, and that you are available to them any time.

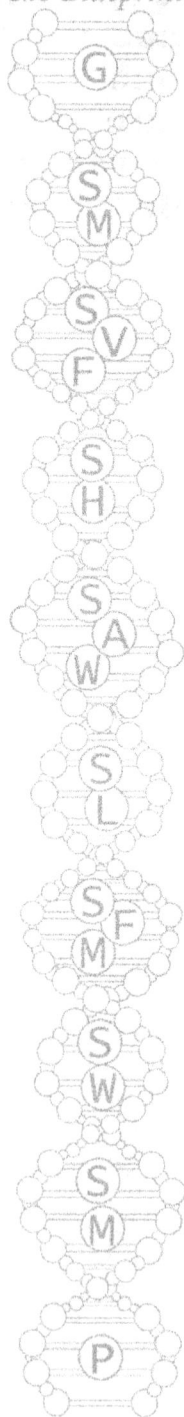

Time to Wake Up

There is a full moon out tonight
and a chill in the air
The atmosphere seems heavy
with a feel of despair
The stillness and quiet
so precious and rare
Allows me to think to look
around and prepare
For what seems to be
inevitable and unfair

What has this world come to,
what have we done?
If we continue this way
we'll destroy everything and everyone
Including our own children,
who we claim to love so much
With our current actions,
we have just put them on deathwatch

Why are we still playing war,
this primitive silly game?
We dramatize our differences,
yet we're all the same
History repeats itself,
but we don't seem to understand
That violence begets more violence
towards us and our fellow man

If we don't realize that our old approach is wrong
Then we haven't come that far,

nor are we bright or strong
It takes courage to study our actions
and collective viewpoint
And rectify our old mistakes with intelligence
not at gunpoint

The current world conflicts
are as old as time itself
We need to find a new game
and put the old one on the shelf
The master players can still have pawns
to move and to control
They can still create effects
with winning as their ultimate goal
But the stakes of the game will change
so it doesn't kill us all

Do we even know what we are truly fighting for?
Destroying all life and burning our planet
down to the core
Our religions, our gods, land
that's mere rocks and sand
Our memes and agreements
that we wear like a brand

Our agreements and reality
are based on a ghetto mentality
Why do we segregate,
when we are all a part of one society?
What if an order plotted to wreak havoc
and cause disorder?
And since they built the initial implant
they possess the decoder

Their mission you see
is to divide and conquer humanity
To manipulate earth's frequency
and control human destiny
Energetically they vibrate
on the level of ego and greed
Their hunger for power
they must constantly feed
To prove to the Light
that they can plant their own seed

They have also created
with great skill and ingenuity
The assortment of
religions, cults, and sects you see
An encoding instrument and symbol
of power had to be
Absolute because total control of the masses
was necessary

One religion is not better
or more sanctified than the next
But we are fighting and killing each other
for our sacred texts
They have all been created
by our brilliant fellow man
In order to dominate and control
or perhaps just because they can

The infamous Messiah that you are all waiting for
Is not some holy great man
who will walk in through the door

It is a mass awakening
that has been hoped for and perceived
By the spiritual masters who have been trained
and have received
Information from the Light
that humanity will be deceived

The human race must use all their spiritual
strength to fight
To keep their freedom and their free will
which is their birthright
But in their effort and inherent desire to be free
They chose to fight each other,
obviously the wrong enemy

You must have all forgotten the power
bestowed upon you
When you assumed a viewpoint
and chose to experience and view
This is a reminder that everyone
and everything you see
Are merely dimension points
consisting of pure energy

They look solid and have significance
because as a group you agree
To keep it in place for this planet's order
and workability
Everything in our reality can be
created, changed, moved, or erased
Simply by adjusting your frequency and
using your willpower always

Humanity this is an urgent wake up call
to all of you
It is time to unite as a race and let your
higher-selves come through
There is great strength in numbers
and with the power of the mind
We can rehabilitate the viewpoints
and frequency of all mankind
Change your lives, your future, and leave
this planet's past behind

~Lana

About the Author

Lana Fuchs is a successful businesswoman, entrepreneur, wife, and mother. Lana resides in Las Vegas with her husband, children, a monkey, a dog, and two cats. Always dancing to her own beat and living according to her own code of ethics, Lana's mantra is, "Believe in yourself, even when no one else does."

www.LanaFuchs.com